Red-Hot Cold Call Selling

Prospecting Techniques That Pay Off

Paul S. Goldner

American Management Association

New York • Atlanta • Boston • Chicago • Kansas City • San Francisco • Washington, D. C.
Brussels • Mexico City • Tokyo • Toronto

Library of Congress Cataloging-in-Publication Data

Goldner, Paul S.
     Red-hot cold call selling: prospecting techniques that pay off /
Paul S. Goldner.
          p.   cm.
     Includes bibliographical references and index.
     ISBN 0-8144-7880-8
     1. Telephone selling.   2. Selling.   I. Title.
HF5438.3.G647   1995
658.8'4—dc20   95-34300
                                                        CIP

Printing number

10   9   8   7   6

Contents

To the girls in my life:
Susan,
Jacqueline,
and
Elissa

Acknowledgments

To Pam Wilson, who gave me my start at AMA.
To Mary Glenn, who believed in my book.
To Jacquie Flynn, for her excellent developmental efforts.
To Mary Dorian of Beehive Production Services, for her excellent copy editing.
To Mike Sivilli for his excellent management skills.
To Judy Lopatin for her great proofreading work.

Preface

I will be selling right up until my last breath. In fact, when I leave this worldly plain, I fully expect to go to heaven. For me, heaven will be a small room with a telephone and a never-ending list of prospects. While this may sound a bit cynical, you cannot succeed at what you do not love. I am going to work very hard on making sure you love to prospect.

Before we begin, I would like to tell you a little bit more about myself. My professional selling career began during graduate school. I'd just completed my first year in the master of business administration program at the William E. Simon Graduate School of Business Administration at the University of Rochester. I was majoring in public accounting and finance. I was searching for a summer job (the university called it an "internship") and wound up with a company that sells wire rope.

For those of you who do not know, wire rope is the cable that holds up bridges. It is also used to raise and lower elevators. It is not the most exciting product in the world and much, if not all, sales activity takes place over the phone. If you are thinking that I was not particularly suited for the job, you are right. I had no formal or informal experience in sales. However, this was the only job opportunity that I had. I took it!

Little did I know what I was in for. I was so petrified that I went the entire summer without making one sale. I did everything I could to avoid picking up the phone. However, I did learn from the experience. Today, I am an entrepreneur. I have two businesses of my own and attribute much of my success to my cold calling prowess. I am so confident in my abilities that I honestly believe I could get an appointment with the president of the United States, should I so desire.

However, my success is no accident. Over the years, through trial and error, experience and study, I have developed a prospecting and business development system that works! This system is outlined in this book. The system includes a number of strategies that will increase your probability of success in the sales cycle.

My recommendations are based on actual experience. I sell. Day in and day out, I sell. Since the mid-1980s, I have done nothing but sell and I will continue to sell until my last day on this earth. Accordingly, these recommendations are not textbook recommendations. Every day, I meet with customers and prospects and the experiences that I have are the same exact ones that you have. I feel the same pressures, fear the same rejections, and have all of the same concerns that you do. Thus, I know my recommendations work!

My experience with prospecting began when I started my first business, a computer training company, in 1983. I had just left a comfortable job with Price Waterhouse, the public accounting giant. When my partner and I opened our business we had no customers and we had no sales.

Our first reaction, being the good accountants we were, was to advertise. My partner and I placed a nice ad in *The New York Times.* We used to fight over who would sit next to our one phone and take the calls. However, a funny thing happened. The phone didn't ring! When you think about pressure, think about this. We had both left cushy jobs at Price Waterhouse and started our own business. I borrowed $3,000 from my father and my partner borrowed the same amount from his wife. We didn't have a large cushion to work with and things were starting out on the wrong foot.

This is where prospecting comes in. Business development is a proactive process. You cannot sit and wait for things to happen. You must go out and make them happen. If you sit and wait for things to happen, you will only expedite your own failure.

My partner and I got on the phone and out in the street. We hustled and built a business. Unfortunately, the recession of the early 1990s burst our bubble. We had built a sales organization for our computer training business by then and had both gotten a little lazy. We had both stopped prospecting. After all, prospecting was not a dignified thing for the president of a success-ful company to do. My role in the company had evolved to our visionary leader.

I had heard a speech about the recession. The speaker's main point was that you need not participate in the recession if you don't want to. Lacking in the speech, however, was the for-mula for success. Naively, I delivered my version of the speech to our sales organization. I declared that while the rest of the country would suffer through this economic downturn, we would not! The recession was just starting to impact the econ-omy and our company, but we were in control of our own des-tiny. While my intentions were certainly honorable, the speech didn't work. Our sales were flat in a high-growth industry. When I looked for ways to increase our sales, the telephone was an obvious choice.

Toward the end of 1991, we began to sit down and pound the phones. At first, nothing seemed to happen and we doubted ourselves. However, we persisted, and 1992 was our best growth year ever, sporting a 62 percent year-over-year growth rate. We attributed our success to a heavy focus on business develop-ment—in other words, prospecting.

I have cold called to sell wire rope, to start a business, and to warm up a recession. However, possibly my best prospecting experience came when we decided to franchise our business. Ours was a conversion program, which means that you must already be in our business to qualify as a franchise prospect. We started the franchise program under a new corporate identity and I was responsible for franchise business development. I had to go to the public library, get the yellow pages for a city that we wished to visit, and start calling to set up appointments.

I would almost like to say that you have not really cold called until you have called out of the yellow pages. While this may not be the single worst list in the world, it certainly ranks quite high. Yet, by employing the strategies outlined in this book, I was able to call into a unfamiliar city, selling an un-known and untested concept, to people I had never met before.

The end result was that I regularly set up six appointments a day, starting at 8:00 A.M. and ending at 6:00 P.M., one appoint-ment every two hours. It was a long day but it worked. Today, our franchise system is the second largest in terms of both sales and locations in the United States.

This book will teach you what prospecting really is and why it is a key element in your selling success formula. You will also learn strategies to overcome the fear of rejection, perhaps the greatest challenge you will face in your journey to selling success. Our goal is to make you "Rejection-Proof."

This book outlines a formula called "Smart Prospecting," a proven method used to establish priorities in the prospecting and sales process. You will be presented with the "Ten Commandments of Prospecting," a strategy that will enhance your probability of success in the sales cycle.

We will dissect a cold call and teach you an effective method for developing your own cold calling script, including not only how to handle your initial conversation but also how to overcome objections and set up subsequent calls to the prospect. Finally, you will be presented with additional strategies that will help you improve upon the likelihood of a positive outcome in the sales cycle, including a "Cold Calling Tool Kit" and a "Reporting and Tracking Tool Kit." We will close by revealing Prospecting's Great Secret!

Let's move on, learn and, most importantly, have fun.

1

Prospecting: An Essential Element to Your Selling Success

Prospecting and business development are possibly the most crucial elements in your selling success formula. Most salespeople realize this. However, most salespeople do not enjoy prospecting and try to minimize the time spent in this area.

As you will see, if you are not successful at prospecting, it's unlikely you'll be a successful salesperson, but if you are, you will undoubtedly be successful in one of the most challenging and rewarding careers this country has to offer. Let's see why.

Steps in the Sales Cycle

A sample sale cycle might have the following steps:

1. Planning
2. Prospecting
3. Meeting
4. Recommending
5. Closing
6. Servicing

Although you will clearly be more effective if you plan your sales activities, planning is not a prerequisite to prospecting. You could always take a copy of the local yellow pages (as I have done), begin with *A*'s, and continue on until you reach the end of your selling career. This strategy will not maximize the return on the time you invest in the sales process, but it will allow you to move forward.

Prospecting, on the other hand, is clearly a prerequisite to the remainder of the selling cycle. If you are not effective at prospecting and business development, you will never have the opportunity to be effective at any remaining element in the sales process. You will never be able to meet prospects, recommend appropriate solutions for their needs, close sales, and provide exceptional postsale customer service.

Given this fact, you could easily conclude that if you are not effective at prospecting, you will not be effective at selling. While the same could be said of any remaining step in the sales cycle, you will clearly reach a premature dead end due to a lack of effectiveness in the prospecting area.

This book is devoted to the fine art of prospecting and business development. Together, we are going travel a path that will completely reengineer your outlook toward business development. As we travel on this journey, one of my goals is to present a few new ideas that will enhance your probability of success in the sales cycle.

Your Path to Success

Enhancing your probability of success in the sales cycle is a crucial point. Sales is a highly competitive business. It should come as no surprise that if you are not calling on your customers and prospects, someone else will be. Accordingly, it is critically important that you obtain every possible edge. During my studies of sales and motivation, I have learned that the differences between the winners and losers, the top performers and the average performers, are not large. Rather, the top performers in a given field are doing things just slightly better than are the others in their profession. In sales, for example, the top producers might make that one extra call or attend that one extra sales meeting. Although the difference in performance is not substantial, the difference in income for the top performers can be significant.

Consider perhaps the greatest golfer of all time. During one year in the 1960s, at or near the peak of his skills, Jack Nicklaus earned approximately $400,000 on the PGA tour. There was another golfer on the PGA tour that year as well. His name was Bob Charles. As a professional Bob Charles was not as successful as Jack Nicklaus. During the same year, Bob Charles earned approximately $40,000 on the PGA tour; the difference in earnings between Bob Charles and Jack Nicklaus was approximately tenfold (excluding income from endorsements and other revenue-generating activities). It might surprise you to learn that the difference in their respective per round stroke averages was less than half a stroke. Imagine that! The difference between the greatest golfer of all time and a very good golfer was less than one-half stroke per round.

This phenomenon takes on even more significance in the world of professional selling. After all, Bob Charles still got paid even if he came in second, third, or tenth. Suppose you are competing with another company for a sale. You submit your proposal and feel as though you have done the very best you can. Further, you feel as though this is one of the very best jobs you have ever done. You call up the prospect to find out his decision. He tells you that you wrote an excellent proposal and did a really great job of understanding his needs. Then he tells you that had it not been for this other company, you would have won the work. Your proposal was second best.

How much revenue does your company earn when you come in second? How much commission do you earn when your company comes in second? The answer to both questions is obvious, which is why it is absolutely crucial that you make every effort to give yourself that competitive edge. The recommendations in this book are designed to do just that—to give you that competitive edge, or to enhance your probability of success in the sales cycle.

My second objective in writing this book is to remind you of certain things that you may have already learned and since forgotten. In fact, I often say that I have forgotten more about professional selling than I remember. In order to keep sharp, I listen to a new audiocassette program each week and read a new book each month. The benefits are astounding!

Recently, I was riding to a Fortune 200 account with one of our account managers. When we arrived, the prospect told us there was no way we would ever do business with his company. The company was happy with its present suppliers.

In the car, however, we had been listening to a Brian Tracy audio program on professional selling. The tape was talking about the instant reverse close. The instant reverse close is designed to ask a question that will completely turn around an apparently dead-end objection. I wasn't sure that either of us were even listening to the program but the message must have gotten through to our subconscious minds.

When faced with the ultimate rejection, the account manager I was with simply asked the prospect what he would do if he were in our shoes and had just heard his response (the instant reverse). He directed us to his manager, the true decision maker in the company. Today, we are doing business with the company.

The point is, we can all learn. I am counting on you to keep both an open mind and, more importantly, to have fun as you learn, my third objective for this book. You see, I love professional selling. In fact, I cannot think of anything I'd rather be doing as far as my career is concerned. It is an exciting job with ample opportunity for financial rewards. Further, selling is extremely challenging. I liken it to a nice round of golf in that you are never presented with the same shot twice, no matter how many times you play the same course. Selling, like golf, presents a unique opportunity each time you meet a prospect or customer.

2

What Is Prospecting?

I am a strong proponent of the idea that in order to be successful at an occupation, you must enjoy what you do. At a minimum, you spend roughly one-third of your adult life at work. How could you possibly be successful if you do not enjoy what you do?

My experience has been that most salespeople love the sales but could live without the prospecting. I, and others, have traced the lack of enthusiasm back to a fear of rejection. This fear can paralyze almost anyone in any profession or endeavor, and often leads to the demise of the salesperson with respect to selling success.

The trick is to alter your perceptions of prospecting, and rejection. We could offer a number of sophisticated psychological techniques to help you. I would prefer to keep it simple and suggest several fun strategies. You can pick the one that works best for you.

Is the Glass Half Full or Half Empty?

Prospecting, like anything else, can be viewed positively or negatively. In other words, is the glass half full or is it half empty? If you believe that the glass is half empty and choose to focus on the rejection involved in prospecting, then it's very easy to see why you might not find prospecting to be an enjoyable part of your job.

On the other hand, there are many positive elements about

prospecting. Viewing the glass as half full will allow you to see prospecting from a completely different, and positive, perspective. Most importantly, you will be taking your first steps toward becoming "Rejection-Proof." Figure 2-1 offers a definition of prospecting that allows us to begin viewing the glass as half full.

Figure 2-1 tells us that prospecting is the conversion of a stack of leads into a stack of money through the effective use of the telephone. Viewing prospecting in this manner allows us to focus on the positive outcome of the process (sales) and leave the negative element (rejection) completely out of our definition. If you take this definition to its logical extreme, it would be hard to think of a better way to earn a living! Imagine another job that allows you to get paid for simply dialing the telephone.

However, as most of us know, it's not quite that easy. After all, our first definition did have the word *effective* as one of its key elements. Being effective is clearly a crucial element to your overall success and is a topic we are going to explore in depth when we discuss "Smart Prospecting." At this point, however, I would like to work with our basic premise a little further.

There is an old story about a man working with a sledge hammer trying to break a large rock. He hits the rock once and nothing happens. He hits it again and nothing happens. He continues by hitting the rock a hundred times without any results. Finally, on the next try, the rock shatters and breaks into many small pieces.

In order to understand this story, one must ask whether the rock broke solely because of the final blow or did it break because of the cumulative effect of all blows. If you are like me, you understand the rock broke because of the cumulative effect. This understanding allows us to further develop our definition of prospecting.

Figure 2-1. Prospecting defined.

The Sun Does Rise in the East and Set in the West

In Chapter 13, we are going to spend a good deal of time discussing how to track your prospecting efforts. Without getting into too much detail at this point, I'd like you to consider the segment of a sample weekly sales report in Figure 2-2. Please note that the information provided in the report is for illustration purposes only.

Here, dials are simply the number of times you pick up the phone and press the number indicated on your lead sheet. Completed calls are the number of times that you actually reach the person you intended to when you initiated the call. This does not include voice mail, or the person's secretary or assistant. The remainder of the definitions—appointments, proposals, sales, and sales $—should be self-explanatory.

The crucial point here is that there is a clear and distinct relationship between the number of times that you dial the phone and the sales volume that you ultimately generate for your company. When we cover reporting and tracking in more detail, we are going to strongly urge that you consider keeping detailed records of your prospecting activities. This will help you to better understand the relationship between dialing the phone and sales volume. Suffice it to say that if you keep accurate records, you will soon learn that your relationship between sales volume and dials of the telephone can be as predictable as the sun rising in the East and setting in the West, irrespective of your prospecting acumen. The tools and ideas presented in this book will simply serve to improve your relationships (between sales volume and dials of the telephone), or, as we said in the first chapter, enhance your probability of success in the sales cycle.

Figure 2-2. Information from a weekly sales report.

Dials	Completed Calls	Appointments	Proposals	Sales	Sales $
100	50	13	13	5	$20,000

What's in It for Me?

I'd like to continue with the example and include one more important point. Please consider the relationship presented in Figure 2-3.

What you should notice is that the relationship we established earlier, between sales volume and dials of the telephone, actually extends beyond that point to a salesperson's commission check—that is, the size of one's commission check is directly related to the number of times one dials the telephone.

Putting a slightly different twist on this observation, one could argue that a salesperson earns money each and every time she dials the telephone, irrespective of the outcome of the call. In this example, the salesperson earns $10 each time she dials the phone. This understanding lies in the fact that one cannot tell, in advance, which calls will be the ones that yield the sales. Therefore, like the person trying to break the rock, it is the cumulative effect of our prospecting efforts that leads to our selling success, not the impact of any given call. This interpretation leads us to the second definition of prospecting as the opportunity to earn income each and every time you dial the telephone.

The chart in Figure 2-4 allows us to take our analysis one step further. What you should notice is that if you increase your level of prospecting activity, your sales volume and ultimately

Figure 2-3. The commission-dialing connection.

Dials	Completed Calls	Appointments	Proposals	Sales	Sales $
100	50	13	13	5	$20,000

Sales	$20,000
Dials	100
Sales/dial	$200
Commission rate	5.00%
Commission/dial	$10

Figure 2-4. More sales report information.

Dials	Completed Calls	Appointments	Proposals	Sales	Sales $
100	50	13	13	5	$20,000
200	100	25	25	10	$40,000
400	200	50	50	20	$80,000

your income increase as well. Hence, prospecting gives you the opportunity to set your level of income.

This definition of prospecting probably accounts for the reason most people enter the world of professional selling. As a salesperson, you have the opportunity to set your level of income. If you wish to increase your level of income, increase your prospecting activity. If (for some reason) you wish to decrease your level of income, decrease your prospecting activity. The results will be very predictable.

Next consider the relationship between prospecting activity and income and how they relate to downturns in the business environment. When the economy enters an economic downturn, or recession, business activity doesn't cease; it simply slows down. The rate at which the economy slows is indicative of the depth of the recession. If you remember, I heard a very clever speech about one's decision to participate in a recession. I thought the speech was so good that I even gave my own interpretation of the facts to our sales organization. What I learned, all too late, was that while the message was right on target, it lacked a specific and definite course of action for follow-up. Through trial and error, and many aggravating days, I finally found the secret. Here it is.

A recession, to a salesperson, simply means that the relationships defined in this chapter are slightly altered. In other words, during a recession, you have to make more calls to yield the same results. But you can still yield those results if you wish. Further, with a small increase in effort, you may even be able to exceed prior performance levels. Not only does prospecting give you the opportunity to set your level of income, but it also gives you the opportunity to determine the extent to which you wish to participate in an economic downturn.

I have heard many stories about salespeople succeeding in a recession far beyond what they had achieved prior to the downturn. Perhaps they understood the ideas outlined in the preceding paragraphs. Couple these ideas with the fact that many of their competitors may have lost their focus, or may have gone out of business, during the same recession and the results can be volatile. After all, most salespeople probably give up during a recession. So while the total pie is smaller, your slice can be proportionately quite a bit larger.

The Law of Sowing and Reaping

I am in the computer training business and have always tried to encourage people to use technology. I might have overstepped my boundaries in trying to impress on my mother, a sales veteran of many years, that automation should be part of her sales arsenal. She told me that salespeople had been selling long before there were computers. In fact, she taught me that references to professional selling actually can be found in the Bible. Let's see where.

The Bible makes reference to the Law of Sowing and Reaping. The Law of Sowing and Reaping tells us, "Whatever ye shall soweth, so shall ye reapeth." As you will soon see, the Law of Sowing and Reaping is a biblical paradigm for professional prospecting and professional selling. In fact, the Law of Sowing and Reaping is the foundation for the relationships outlined previously and lends further credence to the relationship between dials of the telephone, sales volume, and income.

Imagine you were a farmer and planted a crop of only one seed. What type of harvest could you expect down the road? You wouldn't expect to see much of a harvest at all. However, if you planted many seeds, and properly cultivated those seeds, you would typically expect an abundant harvest at the end of the season. Selling, and in particular prospecting, is no different than farming. The seeds that you plant are your cold calls. Plant only one seed, or make only one cold call, and you cannot expect to have an abundant harvest at the end of your sales cycle. However, plant many seeds, or make many cold calls, and like the farmer, you can expect an abundant harvest at the end of your sales cycle.

I am sure that all of us are too familiar with those desperate feelings that often accompany business development and sales. Why didn't they call me back? I have to get that appointment! I need to make this sale! These situations all result in the same uncomfortable, queasy feeling. Each time I get this feeling, I know that I haven't planted enough seeds. The Law of Sowing and Reaping, or planting enough seeds, can be the best remedy for this upset stomach.

Looking at this situation from another perspective can also be quite enlightening. Imagine, as a farmer, you had an abundant harvest. How would you feel? Of course, you would be quite proud of your efforts. However, in light of your abundant harvest, do you think every single seed you planted succeeded? Of course not. There will always be seeds that don't germinate. With an abundant harvest, you probably wouldn't even notice the seeds that didn't grow! That's right—the abundant harvest (your success) has completely overshadowed the fact that certain seeds didn't grow (your failures). If you are successful at prospecting, your successes will overshadow your failures and you will soon learn that there is no better way to earn a living.

A Positive Outlook

Napoleon Hill, the author of *Think and Grow Rich,* once said that there are three sides to every story: my side, your side, and the correct side, which probably lies somewhere in between. There is great wisdom in these words. Some, including myself, would argue that prospecting is great fun. Others would argue that it is not. Prospecting can be fun if you give it a chance. Remember, prospecting not only gives you the opportunity to earn money each and every time you dial the telephone; it also gives you the opportunity to set your level of income. Prospecting is also quite challenging. What more could you want in a career?

Now that we have a positive outlook on the prospecting process, let's move on to the next chapter and learn why prospecting is an essential element in your business development success formula.

3

Why Prospect?

A Day in the Life of a Sales Professional

I'd like to reflect again on my first sales position: the summer internship I had selling wire rope. Like all hardworking sales professionals, I would get to work by 8:00 A.M. My experience now tells me that the hour between 8:00 and 9:00 A.M. is one of the best times to prospect. This is particularly true today with the advent of voice mail. However, youth is wasted on the young, as the saying goes. My typical workday would start with an hour of coffee drinking, newspaper reading, and talking with the other folks in the company. No calls were made.

I would then move on to one of professional selling's greatest rituals: "Lead Sorting." This practice involves taking your leads and sorting them so that they are in the best possible order to begin your day's work. It is not clear to me why we engage in this curious behavior as lead sorting has no direct, measurable impact on success in the sales process. Yet, most salespeople, if not all of us, sort our leads into the best possible order prior to beginning prospecting for the day. My lead sorting routine would always take an hour or two, from 9:00 to 11:00. The end result was that I made no calls. By 11:00, I was faced with a grave dilemma.

I assumed that all of my prospects were preparing to go to lunch. Being polite, I did not want to interrupt their preparation process, so I made no calls between 11:00 and noon. I also assumed that my prospects were out to lunch between noon and

2:00. Not wanting to waste time on the phone if no one would be available, I made no calls during the lunch hours either.

After lunch was also no time for prospecting. After all, your prospects had just returned from a fulfilling meal and you did not want to give them indigestion. Being the consummate professional, I gave my prospects one hour to digest their lunch, from 2:00 to 3:00.

Finally, I closed out my day from 3:00 to 5:00. I must share with you that I was thoroughly exhausted at this point. I had come to work at 8:00 and I had done nothing but prospecting and business development (or so I thought) up until 3:00. I used the last hours of my day to wrap up and I allowed my prospects to do the same. At 5:00 P.M. I left. As you can see, the end result of this sophisticated process was that I made no calls. The Law of Sowing and Reaping tells us that this places us in a very precarious position as sales professionals. If we do not make cold calls, we will have done little, if anything, to further our business development efforts.

Just Do It

Nike has a great motto that you see all over television these days: "Just Do It!" As a professional salesperson, you have basically two functions. Your first responsibility is to service your existing customers. Your second responsibility is toward business development. This is what you are paid to do. When you are not providing superior customer service, you must devote your full attention and energy to business development and prospecting. It is crucial to your selling success.

As we all know, it is just too easy to avoid prospecting. I was very successful at avoiding my business development responsibilities in my first sales job and it showed by virtue of the fact that I made no sales. Since it is so difficult to motivate yourself to prospect, I'd like to explore several *compelling reasons to prospect.*

First, most prospects never receive the information you send. I would like to be able to reference a sophisticated research study to support my conclusion in this area. Unfortunately, I can only back up my statement with personal experience and the experience of almost everyone I have taught. When you send unsolicited information in the mail, one of six outcomes are possible:

1. Prospect never received the information for a variety of reasons.
2. Prospect received the information and threw it in the garbage.
3. Prospect received the information, read it, and threw it in the garbage.
4. Prospect received the information, read it, and passed it on to someone else.
5. Prospect received the information, read it, and saved it for a later date.
6. Prospect received the information, read it, and called you.

Unfortunately, the least likely outcome is the last one. Most prospects do not respond to the information we send. Prospecting is our opportunity, as salespeople, to be *proactive* instead of reactive. I'm sure that many of you have read Stephen Covey's excellent book, *The Seven Habits of Highly Effective People.* Habit One is the Habit of Proactivity. Proactivity places you in control of your own destiny, a primary motivation to join the profession of selling in the first place. I prefer to send information to support a phone call, not to pave the way for one. The difference is subtle but will decrease the length of your sales cycle by several weeks at a minimum.

Second, most people rise to challenges and prospecting is quite challenging. In telephone prospecting, you have two to three minutes to convince a complete stranger to spend some of his valuable time with you. As most of us have learned, this situation can be quite a challenge. However, as we all know, it is very rewarding when you get the appointment. The reason getting the appointment can be so rewarding is because prospecting is a microcosm of the sales process. How do you feel when you make a sale? You feel great! Why? Because you reached a goal. The goal of a prospecting call is to get an appointment. When you get an appointment, you have reached your goal and should feel elated. In fact, you should feel no less elated than when you make a sale. Why? Because you just made one! You sold someone on the concept of spending some of his valuable time with you.

Third, your prospecting success will breed additional prospecting success. Have you ever heard the saying, "Strike while the iron is hot"? Reflect for a moment on the elation you feel when you get that key appointment at a major account. You feel great! You're on top of the world! It has been said that selling is the transfer of enthusiasm about your product or service from you to the buyer, because if the buyer feels as strongly about your product or service as you do, a sale will occur. When you feel great, you are more likely to be successful in your next prospecting call. That's right. Immediately after making that key appointment, get right back on the phone and make some more. Your enthusiasm will be contagious and your probability of success will soar. Strike while the iron is hot!

Next, prospecting prevents the selling peaks and valleys from which most salespeople seem to suffer. Some peaks and valleys can be attributed to the seasonality of a business, but most can be attributed to inconsistent prospecting efforts. In Chapter 2, we learned about a strong relationship between the number of times you dial the phone and your sales volume. A consistent diet of prospecting calls will yield a consistently successful sales career just as a consistent diet of healthy food will lead to a long and healthy life.

Finally, and most importantly, prospecting is fun. Prospecting and selling are fun! After all, where else can you get paid to talk on the phone, meet people, and serve their needs? Selling is a great profession and you should relish your opportunity to be one of its proud members.

4

Becoming Rejection-Proof

In Chapter 3, I shared with you an in-depth account of my first experience with professional selling. I had a very sophisticated daily routine. I hate to admit it, but the entire routine was developed with one goal in mind: I did not want to make any cold calls. At the time, all I knew was that I was petrified. I didn't know why. Now I know that I suffered from a tremendous fear of rejection.

I suspect that if we all sold long enough, we would eventually overcome our fear of rejection. From my perspective, I'm not sure why we should wait twenty years or so for this to happen. I'd like to offer a strategy that can help you overcome your fear of rejection now: the "Selling Life-Cycle Paradigm."

Educating Your Prospects

A paradigm is simply a way of looking at something. The Selling Life-Cycle Paradigm teaches you to view sales as a process and not as an event. The goal of the sales process according to the Selling Life-Cycle Paradigm is to educate your prospects and customers. In other words, if your prospects knew exactly what you knew about your product or service and felt exactly as you felt about your product or service, they would buy.

More specifically, selling is the process of educating your prospects about the value your product or service will add to the profitability of their organization. If you can demonstrate that your product or service will yield a superior return on their investment, they will buy. If you cannot, then you must return the prospect to the sales pipeline and continue the education process at a later point in time.

Once you can demonstrate that your product or service will yield a superior return on investment, you will have a customer. Continue to demonstrate that your product or service will yield a superior return on investment and you will have a customer for life. However, the onus is on you to demonstrate the value you bring to the table, which is why I believe that selling is a lifelong education process. If the prospect does not buy, you simply have to do a better job in the education area.

Continuing the Selling Process

One can never be rejected as long as the selling process continues. By being persistent, by continuing the education process, and by repositioning your prospect to an appropriate position in your sales pipeline after a temporary setback in the sales cycle, you have the ability to control the ultimate outcome of the sales process and the ability to control any emotions associated with an apparent rejection. In fact, given this perspective of selling, you see that it is impossible to lose a sale. The Selling Life-Cycle Paradigm is further explained in Figure 4-1.

Most salespeople realize they need sales today. Most will

Figure 4-1. The selling life-cycle paradigm.

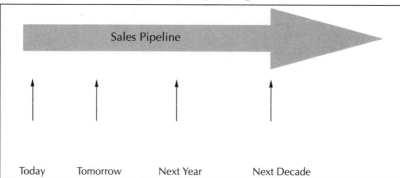

also realize that they need sales tomorrow. What few salespeople realize is that they also need sales one year from today and one decade from today if they plan on remaining in the field of professional selling. By viewing sales as a process and not as an event, our "NO's" today plant the seeds for "YES's" one year from today and ten years from today. Following this thought process, a rejection should never be viewed as a no. Rather, a rejection should simply be viewed as information about a given prospect that both allows you to properly position that prospect in your sales pipeline and focus the direction of your education process. This concept is illustrated in Figure 4-2.

The Selling Life-Cycle Paradigm also teaches us that there is little, if anything, you can do to force a prospect to buy. Therefore, we can maximize our return on investment by rapidly finding those prospects who are ready, willing, and able to buy now, while repositioning those who are not to an appropriate place in our sales pipeline.

In the next chapter, entitled "Smart Prospecting," we are going to discuss how to properly define our target market. You will learn that once prospects are in your target market, there will be no way for them to leave because your target market will be defined based on objective, quantitative criteria, not emotion. Therefore, a NO! today leaves you with no alternative but to reposition the prospect to an appropriate, new place in your sales pipeline. As long as your prospects meet the criteria that

Figure 4-2. Rejection as part of the sales process.

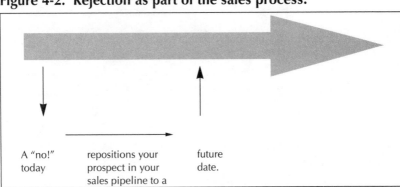

A "no!"   repositions your   future
today   prospect in your   date.
               sales pipeline to a

define your target market, they must remain in the sales pipeline, irrespective of the outcome of your last call to them. The emotion or rejection has been replaced with an objective, quantifiable criterion.

I'd like to illustrate this point with an example. Not too long ago, one of our salespeople came to me looking a little disturbed and wondering what to do. He had just received a letter from Jan, one of his prospects in his target market, and wanted to discuss it with me. The letter said that we should stop calling the account, stop sending letters to the account, and remove the company from our mailing list. In fact, Jan wrote that we would never do business with the prospect account as long as she was the decision maker. The salesperson wanted to know what to do.

As I ripped up the letter, I referred the salesperson to the Selling Life-Cycle Paradigm: sales is a process, not an event. In fact, sales is an education process and my interpretation of this event was that we simply had not done a good enough job in educating this prospect on the benefits of working with our organization.

The salesperson wanted to know why I was ripping up the letter. I replied, when you call the prospect the next time, you will not remember how rude she had been to you. We simply removed the rejection element from the equation, focused on the facts (that is, that the prospect was still in our target market based on our established criteria), and continued the sales process. Although we are still not doing business with the account today, I would suspect that the company is farther along in the sales cycle than if we had stopped trying the day we received the letter. In fact, this is one area that you get that competitive edge we were talking about in Chapter 1. It is pretty clear what our chances of doing business with the account would have been had we stopped the sales and education process when we received the letter. By continuing the education process over the last several years, our chances must have improved ever so slightly. The point to understand is that if you improve your probability of success on the margin over a large number of accounts, by believing in the Selling Life-Cycle Paradigm, you will have a tremendous impact on your success as a salesperson. Remember, the difference between Jack Nicklaus and Bob Charles was less than half a stroke per round.

Persistence Pays Off

I'm sure you have heard over and over again that most sales are made after the fifth sales call, yet most salespeople quit after the first call. In my opinion, the reason we quit can be traced back to our fear of rejection. Persistence, or not quitting after the first rejection, is one of the qualities that define not only successful salespeople, but successful people in general. We are going to discuss the virtue of persistence in depth when we learn about the "Ten Commandments of Prospecting," but it may pay at this point to reflect upon some of the great examples of persistence that permeate our history books.

Many of us have heard how Abraham Lincoln lost every election but one prior to his being elected president of the United States. Where would he (and the United States) have wound up if it were not for his persistence?

Many of us have also read how Thomas Edison failed more than ten thousand times prior to inventing the incandescent light. However, Edison's view of failure can shed interesting light on the word *persistence*. Rather than failing, he believed that he succeeded in finding ten thousand ways not to invent the incandescent light. In other words, the process of elimination is a vital part of the invention process. Edison went on to say that he knew he would soon succeed because he ran out of ways that didn't work. Where would we be today if it were not for Edison's great persistence?

More recent history also points to great examples of persistence. Colonel Sanders was rejected more than a thousand times before his first successful sale of the Kentucky Fried Chicken formula. Lee Iacocca was fired from the presidency of Ford Motor Company but his persistence led him on to even greater heights as the chairman of Chrysler Corporation.

Thomas Watson, the founder of IBM, when asked about how others could emulate his great success formula, replied simply to increase your rate of failure. In other words, trying and failing is a risk one must bear in order to be able to try and succeed. Why? Because failure and rejection are necessary precursors to your success. However, Watson's formula only works when combined with one additional special ingredient— persistence.

You cannot lose the game if you control when it ends. Viewing selling as a process and not an event allows you to control the end of the game. Make sure it ends only after you convert the prospect to a satisfied client.

I've often said, "It's only a matter of time before everyone in the world will do business with me." While I might sound a little overconfident, I'm simply reinforcing the Selling Life-Cycle Paradigm. I control when the game ends, I persist, I continue to educate my prospects, and ultimately they will understand the superior value my product or service brings to their organization.

Overcoming the Fear of Rejection Through Diversification

In Chapter 2 we discussed the Law of Sowing and Reaping. This law suggested that whatever we soweth, so shall we repeath. When we expanded this definition to cover prospecting, we learned that our cold calls are the seeds that we plant at the beginning of the sales cycle. Plant only one seed and your whole harvest depends on the outcome of that one seed. Make only one cold call and your whole selling career depends on the outcome of that one cold call. If your whole selling career depends on the outcome of only one call, it becomes quite clear why prospecting can be a great source of anxiety for the salesperson. Hence, the fear of rejection.

The key to removing this anxiety or fear lies in the fact that you must make enough prospecting calls so that the outcome of one call is not and cannot be significant to your overall selling results. This strategy is not new in business but it may not have received its just due in selling. The strategy is called *diversification.*

In the financial community, mutual funds were created to

achieve diversification. Invest in one stock, and your financial well-being rests with the fortunes of just one company as the stock price either goes up or down. A mutual fund, in contrast, is a collection of stocks. In fact, it's typically a large collection of stocks. The theory behind mutual fund investing is that the movement in any one stock has very little impact on the overall results of the fund. In other words, you have diversified away your risk. If you feel that investing in one mutual fund is still too risky, you could diversify even more by investing in several mutual funds, further reducing the effect any one stock could have on your overall financial performance.

Prospecting can work in exactly the same manner. As you increase the number of cold calls you make, the outcome of any one call has less and less significance. Couple this strategy with the Selling Life-Cycle Paradigm—which suggests that it's only a matter of time before every prospect will do business with you—and you should be able to remove prospecting anxiety and the fear of rejection completely from your vocabulary.

Applying the theory of diversification to your day-to-day selling activities can be very revealing. In Chapter 2, we defined a relationship between dials of the telephone and sales volume. I told you that this relationship was as predictable as the sun rising in the East and setting in the West. The reason I can be so sure of this relationship is because it is based on the Law of Large Numbers. In fact, the entire insurance industry, and the entire selling profession, is based on this same law. Actuaries can tell you how many males in the State of New York between the ages of twenty-five and thirty-five will have a car accident this year. The thing they cannot tell you is which ones. Prospecting works in exactly the same manner. Using myself as an example, I know that I will get one appointment, on average, every ten times I dial the phone. Remember, a dial is defined as simply pressing the seven-digit phone number and letting the phone ring. What I can't tell you is who the appointments will be with.

Please keep in mind that this does not mean I get one appointment each and every time I make ten dials. Sometimes I get more and sometimes I get none. On average, though, I do get one in ten, and I can bank on it. Because I understand that over the long run I will achieve the results that I am looking for, one rejection, or many rejections, has no impact whatsoever on my mental attitude.

You, too, have your own ratio that you can bank on. This is the most compelling reason to keep track of your prospecting activities. So, if you ever fear rejection, if you ever have anxiety surrounding the cold calling process, understand that the source of your anxiety stems from the simple fact that you are not making enough calls. You are violating the Law of Sowing and Reaping and the Law of Large Numbers. The good news is, now you have a cure for your anxiety: Make more calls!

Believe in Your Product; Believe in Yourself

Before we close this chapter, I have two final thoughts on rejection-proof prospecting. First, I have taught professional selling to thousands of students over the years. While the names, faces, companies, and products change, there is always one constant. Virtually everyone I have ever taught firmly believes they are benefitting their customer or prospect by selling them their product or service. In other words, they believe in their product or service. If they didn't believe in their product or service, they would have great difficulty being successful and would have likely moved on to another sales position.

If you believe in your product or service, each time you make a sale you are making your customer better off. If you believe that your customers are better off for having done business with you, doesn't it make sense that your prospects will also be better off? Of course it does! Keep this in mind during the prospecting process. Most salespeople believe they are being a bother to the prospects by repeatedly calling to arrange for an appointment. If you believe in your product or service, your perspective should be just the opposite. You should feel as though you have an obligation to call your prospects. Remember, you are selling a good, improving the prospect's position by making a purchase with you. Knowing that you are providing a much needed product or service to the marketplace should enhance your confidence and hence move you closer to our goal of becoming rejection-proof.

Finally, remember that you cannot lose what you never had, so let's not lament the seeds that do not grow. Rather, let's move on to the next chapter, "Smart Prospecting," which will add to our rejection-proof strategies as well as teach us how to work smarter, not harder.

5

Smart Prospecting

We have talked quite a bit about maximizing your return on investment as a sales professional. In order to do this, we must understand that all salespeople are created equal. In other words, we are all given the same commodity to invest each and every day: time. Not only are we given the same commodity with which to trade, but we are all given equal amounts: twenty-four hours in a day. It stands to reason that a salesperson who invests his or her time most wisely will receive the highest return on his or her investment. In fact, the name of the game in selling, and in business, is to maximize your return on investment. For a salesperson, return on investment is calculated as:

$$\text{Return on investment} = \frac{\text{Sale}}{\text{Time invested in the sale}}$$

This chapter is designed to teach you how to maximize your return on investment.

Fishing for Whales

In Chapter 1, we reviewed a sample sales cycle. The sales cycle included planning, prospecting, meeting, recommending, closing, and servicing. When we reviewed the sales cycle, we noted that you could start the sales cycle at step 2, the prospecting step, without considering step 1, the planning step. While this is true, I strongly suggest that planning should be a necessary precursor to prospecting. Here's why. The equation tells us that a salesperson's return on investment is calculated by taking the value of a sale and dividing it by the time invested in the sale.

I now suggest that the time invested in a sale is typically constant. Therefore, in order to maximize your return on investment, you will have to maximize the magnitude of your sale. In other words, in order to maximize your return on investment as a salesperson, you must find those buyers of your products and services that are most likely to make major purchases. To illustrate my point, let's consider two car buyers: one a wealthy buyer looking to purchase a Rolls Royce, and the other, a middle-class buyer looking to borrow money to purchase a moderate car that will be paid off over a three-year period.

The wealthy buyer will likely purchase the car without too much investigation. Why? First, the purchase is not that significant to the wealthy buyer. Second, a Rolls Royce has an assumed level of quality.

On the other hand, the middle-class buyer will probably invest many hours understanding her purchase decision. Why? The purchase is very significant to the middle-class buyer. It is one she will have to live with for three years. Second, given her limited resources, the middle-class buyer will likely investigate the purchase in greater detail to make certain she is maximizing her return on investment.

This example would argue that smaller purchasers invest more time in a purchase decision than do large buyers. This is probably true for individual purchasers. But what about corporate purchasers? Would they follow the same rule of thumb?

Corporations are in business to make money, or to continue with the Return-on-Investment Paradigm, to maximize their return on investment. Given this fact, I would like to suggest that corporate purchasers, with a mandate to maximize their return on investment, will invest the same amount of time in a purchase decision, irrespective of the size of the purchase. After all, have you ever worked with someone who said, "Don't be concerned with doing a good job for us since we are only a small purchaser of your product or service"? Of course not.

The key point to understand in our return-on-investment equation is if the time you must invest in a sale is typically going to be constant irrespective of the size of the sale, in order to maximize your return on investment, you must maximize the size of the sale. This brings us to the first rule in smart prospecting: Fish for whales, not for minnows!

After presenting this unique way of viewing the purchase decision in many seminars, I often hear an objection from seminar participants who say fishing for whales is akin to "putting all of your eggs in one basket." That is, if you only have a few large accounts, and you lose one, you will lose a significant portion of your income. However, you can mitigate this risk by having more than a few large accounts, which is the benefit of account diversity and the Law of Sowing and Reaping discussed in Chapter 2.

The Sales Portfolio

In the field of investing, a portfolio is the collection of all of your stocks. In the field of professional selling, a portfolio is the collection of all of your customers or accounts. When you make investments, you get to set the level of risk you wish to bear. If you wish to bear more risk, you invest in fewer stocks. If you wish to bear less risk, you invest in more stocks, thus diversifying away some of your risk.

The same can be said of your sales portfolio. You get to set your level of risk! If you wish to have a high-risk portfolio, you make investments in fewer accounts. If you wish to have a lower-risk portfolio, you can also diversify away a portion of your risk by investing in more accounts. In other words, there is no reason to believe that you can only manage a few large accounts. You can manage as many as you wish, thus setting the level of risk you wish to bear. How do you find these large accounts? Well, that's exactly where prospecting and Smart Prospecting come in!

Defining Your Target Market

The first step in Smart Prospecting involves defining your target market. Most salespeople might define their target market as "all companies that purchase our product or service." If you work within a region, you might further refine your definition to focus on your region only.

The concern with the previous definition is the word *all.* The word *all* implies a lack of focus. Remember, our goal as salespeople is to maximize our return on investment, and we can only accomplish this goal by finding those buyers of our product or service who are most likely to make major purchases. Although it might seem as though you are limiting your opportunities by excluding some buyers from your target market, you are not. What you are doing is setting your priorities so that you work with the largest and most likely buyers in your market first. You can always expand your target market definition at a later time to include additional buyers. However, you would only want to expand after you have first worked with all potential buyers in your initial target market definition. My experience has been that if you properly define your target market, there will be sufficient opportunity within your target market so that it will not be worth your while to look outside your target market. The opportunities outside of your target market will simply be too small. More importantly, you will have maximized the return you receive on the time you invest in the sales process.

Instead of defining your target market with the word *all,* you might consider defining your target market based on a demographic factor. The demographic factor you select should clearly be the one that best describes the buying potential of your target market. Examples might be sales, locations, number of employees, and net worth. For example, by selecting all companies with more than a hundred employees or all individuals with net worths in excess of $100,000, you will have separated the large buyers of your product or service from the smaller buyers. In selecting your demographic factor, you should consider one that is easily obtained. After all, you do not want to spend all of your time doing research and none of your time selling.

You might be wondering where does one obtain the necessary demographics to perform the exercise of Smart Prospecting. Whenever you are searching for information, you can always find it from one of two sources: purchased sources and free sources. Great examples of purchased information include Dun & Bradstreet, A. C. Nielsen, and other companies that sell information for a living. The big benefit of purchased information is that someone else has taken the time to cull through countless mounds of data and refined the data into an immediately useful format for the salesperson. The big detriment to purchased information is it requires financial resources that might not be available to the salesperson.

There are also a number of sources of free information, including the local Chamber of Commerce, the public library, and your city's trade or business publication. The major benefit of free information is that it does not require a financial investment in order to be of use. The major detriment is that it does require a significant investment in time to raise the quality of the free information to the level of purchased information.

The decision one is faced with is, once again, where will I obtain my greatest return on investment? Where the financial resources exist, my personal bias would be for purchased information. I believe that purchasing good information and focusing your efforts on selling will usually lead to a higher return on investment. Where the purchased information is not a likely alternative, using free information and sifting through it using your human capital will serve as a nice surrogate.

Continuing with our example and assuming that the number of employees is the demographic factor that best describes your target market, you could fine-tune the definition of your target market from "all companies that could use our product or service" to "all companies with more than a hundred employees that could use our product or service." We have made the decision that a hundred employees separates the large purchasers from the smaller purchasers since our demographic factor is designed to quantify the buying potential of prospects within our target market.

An additional benefit to this approach is that residence in your target market is now determined by an objective criterion, not your feelings toward the prospect. In other words, as long as the prospect has a hundred or more employees, it remains in your target market and you must continue to cultivate the relationship. Alternatively, if you have a poorly defined target market, rejection often will serve as a surrogate for your demographic factor, which means that your feelings toward the prospect, not buying potential, determines how you set your priorities. I would like to suggest that buying potential—the objective criterion—not feelings toward the prospect derived from numerous rejections—the subjective criterion—be the determining factor in how you set priorities within your target market. This will serve to make you rejection-proof, since your emotions will now be removed from the equation, and will maximize your return on investment since you are basing your decisions on buying potential.

If you reflect back to the Selling Life-Cycle Paradigm, you will now better understand why "It's just a matter of time before everyone in the world will do business with you!" By defining your target market as any company with a hundred or more employees, you, as the salesperson, cannot decide whether or not a company qualifies for your target market. An objective demographic factor is the controlling variable. Therefore, a company or individual cannot reject itself out of your target market. Only a change in the demographic factor can. Combine the Selling Life-Cycle Paradigm with a healthy dose of persistence and you'll be on your way to prospecting success.

Another benefit of defining your target market in a quantitative fashion is the benefit of focus. Les Brown, the famous motivational speaker, says that you are either moving toward your goals or away from them. There is no in-between because even if you are standing still, the rest of the world is moving forward. Hence, you are being left behind. By defining your target market in a quantitative manner, there is no doubt whether a prospect is in or out. This allows you to focus only on those accounts that are in your target market. In other words, you're always moving toward your goal of maximizing your return on investment because you are working only with the largest buyers of your product or service in the marketplace.

Our analysis, thus far, is strictly quantitative, very black and white. However, there are two additional factors that you may want to consider when formulating your target market: geography and one additional demographic factor. Geography is important in many industries. If this is true in your industry, the closer you are to a customer, the more likely you are to do business with him. This factor probably relates back to your ability to service the customer and the customer's desire to see who he is doing business with. If your business is one in which proximity to the customer plays a role in the decision-making process, you may want to consider adding a geographic dimension to your definition of a target market. Continuing with our example, the definition of your target market could then be modified to be "all companies within 100 miles of our office and with more than a hundred employees that could use our product or service."

I also said that you may want to add one additional demographic factor, such as the region's list of fastest-growing companies, into your definition of a target market to allow for some flexibility. There are certain accounts in every market that are deemed to be "strategic" and you don't want to construct your definition so as to be too rigid to exclude those companies. Strategic accounts could be the region's list of fastest-growing companies or Fortune 2000 companies with locations in your geographic region no matter what the size. The reason the former might be considered strategic is because although these companies may not be in your target market today based on your original target market definition, they may be the giants of tomorrow, so you may want to consider working with them now. The reason the latter might be considered strategic is because of your ability to leverage the relationship and use them as a reference at other accounts in your target market. Saying you do business with AT&T lends a great deal of credibility to a sales presentation. The one concern with adding an additional element to your definition of a target market is that you must be careful not to dilute your focus. Otherwise, you'll wind up back to the *all* definition and lose your ability to set priorities. Concluding our example, our final target market definition might be "all companies within 100 miles of our office and with more than a hundred employees, or any company on our region's list of fifty fastest-growing companies, irrespective of how many employees they currently have, that could use our product or service."

In summary, notice that the definition of our target market includes the following elements:

- A quantitative element based on a known demographic factor
- A geographic element based on proximity to your office (if applicable)
- One additional quantitative element, used for strategic purposes, to provide for limited flexibility

Segmenting Your Target Market

Once you have defined your target market, the next step is to segment your market into three categories: high-priority accounts, moderate-priority accounts, and low-priority accounts. The goal is to further refine your target market so that you place the greatest emphasis on those prospects who are most likely to buy the largest quantities of your product or service. This will, of course, result in maximizing your return on investment.

Your priorities should again be based on the demographic and geographic factors selected previously. For example, our target market could be stratified as follows:

- *High-priority accounts:* Any account with more than 250 employees within 50 miles of our office.
- *Moderate-priority accounts:* Any account with 100 to 250 employees within 50 miles of our office or any account with more than 250 employees farther than 50 miles from our office.
- *Low-priority accounts:* Any account with 100 to 250 employees farther than 50 miles from our office.

The reason for stratifying your market is that you can now set call and visit goals for each account so as to place your greatest emphasis on those accounts that will maximize your return on investment. Again, referring to the Selling Life-Cycle Paradigm, the approach of stratifying your target market will ensure that you minimize the time between calls to your largest accounts. This will, in turn, ensure that the largest potential accounts are consistently being placed into your sales pipeline.

Before discussing why and how to set call and visit goals it is appropriate to discuss what happens to accounts outside of your target market. For example, suppose a company with fifty employees calls up to place an order. Should you accept the order? The answer to this question is a resounding "YES." However, the reason for the answer is that the company called you; you did not make the call. For accounts outside of your target market, I would suggest a less expensive strategy than face-to-face selling. These smaller accounts might be the target of a direct-mail campaign, for example. I would not recommend making them the focus of your telemarketing and face-to-face selling efforts since they will not yield a return on investment sufficient to justify your efforts. A direct-mail program, with a lower investment per contact, may be sufficient to address this segment of the marketplace.

Goals for Your Target Market

I would now like to address how to set appropriate call and visit goals for each of your three target market segments. In general, for goals to be effective as motivational devices, they must be achievable and within the control of the salesperson. The strength of call and visit goals, when compared to sales goals, are that call and visit goals are largely within the control of the salesperson, whereas sales goals often are not. Each day, you can fully control the number of prospecting calls that you make. To a lesser extent you can also control the number of client and prospect visits you make, largely by controlling your call activity. The decision to buy, however, is largely out of your hands. An example of how one might set call and visit goals for each category of account in your target market follows:

High-priority accounts:	One call per month, one face-to-face visit per quarter
Moderate-priority accounts:	One call per quarter, one face-to-face visit per half year
Low-priority accounts:	One call per half year, one face-to-face visit per year

Winning With Smart Prospecting

The key point to understand is that your call and visit goals must reflect the priorities you established when you stratified your target market. The end result should be a prospecting plan that leaves no doubt what you, as a salesperson, must do in order to achieve market success.

The final rule in Smart Prospecting is to make as many calls as possible. This might sound like a contradiction because quality calls should always be preferred to quantity calls. However, because we have taken the time to qualify and quantify our target market, each call we make is, by definition, a quality call. Therefore, the only remaining variable is quantity, or how much effort do you want to place into your selling success.

At this point, you probably understand that Smart Prospecting is an element of Strategic Selling designed to maximize your return on investment. In the next chapter, we are going to learn about the Ten Commandments of Prospecting, a series of additional prospecting strategies that will enhance our probability of success in the sales cycle.

6

The Ten Commandments
of Prospecting

Prospecting can be much like going to the health club. It's something that you know is good for you and will produce excellent and predictable results, yet it's something that most salespeople always seem to avoid. When I reflect back on my first selling position, I was always busy but never seemed to prospect and, hence, never seemed to sell. What we are going to propose in this chapter is a simple ten-step system that will help you in the prospecting process. While each step in the system may not seem to break new ground, it is the system itself that yields tremendous results.

A system is simply a proven methodology for accomplishing a goal. Years ago, I had a goal of losing some weight. I tried dieting on my own but was not successful. I then joined the Weight Watchers Weight Loss Program, followed their system, and was very successful. The difference in results was due to the difference in the system. The interesting thing about the Weight Watchers System is that it worked with an amazing degree of accuracy and predictability. Those that followed the system lost weight; those that didn't, had less success.

A further interesting observation is that only slight modifications to the system seemed to destroy its effectiveness. In other words, in order for the system to work, it must be followed to the letter. Once you start to add your own ingredients, you start to upset the fine balance upon which the system was developed. For example, one small element of the Weight Watchers System is that participants are asked to record their daily food intake in detail. Now you might wonder what record keeping has to do with weight loss. However, there was an amazingly high degree of correlation between weight loss and those who kept accurate records! Those that followed the system and recorded their food intake, lost weight. Those that did not follow the system and did not record their food intake, seemed to never lose weight.

The only way I can account for this observation is that we all report to a higher authority. In the area of weight loss, we can call that higher authority the "Great God of the Scale." Unfortunately, the Great God of the Scale is always watching, even when you are not recording your food intake. As such, I am certain that those who did not lose weight, did not keep accurate records of their food intake. However, the Great God of the Scale did keep accurate records and made certain that they did not lose weight at the end of the week. The key point is that the Weight Watchers' system includes record keeping. If you want the system to work for you, accurate record keeping must be part of the program. There can be no compromise.

Just like there is a Great God of the Scale, there is also a Great God of the Sale who watches your prospecting and selling activity. Follow the rules set forth by the Great God of the Sale and your results will be very predictable: you will be a selling superstar. Violate those rules, and you proceed at your own risk. The Ten Commandments of Prospecting is a proven success formula for prospecting and selling success.

COMMANDMENT 1:   Make an appointment with yourself for one hour each day to prospect.

Prospecting requires discipline. Prospecting can always be put off until a later day when the circumstances will be better. I can assure you that the time will never be exactly right to prospect. Make an appointment each day to prospect. Prospecting should be placed on the same priority level as a meeting with a client or potential client or a meeting with your boss. Write the appointment into your time management system and *do it!* Prospecting is so important to me that I even do it on my car phone. This is often the only time I have to myself during the day. Although some might consider this practice extravagant, if I make one additional appointment each month I believe that I receive a very generous return on my investment.

COMMANDMENT 2: Make as many calls as possible.

Smart Prospecting taught us only to call the best prospects in the market. Therefore, every call we make has the potential to be a quality call, since we are only calling those prospects who are most likely to buy large quantities of our product or service. Make as many calls as possible during the hour. Since every call is a quality call, more is always preferred to less.

I've often been asked do I take calls during my prospecting hour. The answer is a resounding "NO!" While prospecting, my phone is always on DND (Do Not Disturb) and my door is always closed. If you set aside one hour a day for prospecting, make certain that you make one full hour of calls. Any distractions will only serve to dilute your efforts. Remember, the Great God of the Sale is always watching and will reward you only on the basis of the Law of Sowing and Reaping, not on the Law of Intending to Sow.

COMMANDMENT 3: Make your calls brief.

The objective of the prospecting call is to get the appointment. You cannot sell a complex product or service over the phone and you certainly don't want to get into a debate of some sort. Your prospecting call should last approximately two to three minutes and should be focused on introducing yourself, your product, briefly understanding the prospects' needs so that you can provide them with a very good reason to spend some of their valuable time with you, and most importantly, getting the appointment.

If you reflect on the strategy outlined in the previous chapter, you should see that your job as a professional salesperson is to find those prospects who are ready, willing, and able to buy now as fast as possible, while repositioning the remaining prospects in your target market to an appropriate spot in your sales pipeline. Given that you are trying to find those prospects who are ready to buy now as fast as possible, a rejection at this point in the sales cycle should be viewed as a positive event in that it allows you to reposition the current prospect to a later point in your sales pipeline, while now moving on to other prospects who might bear more immediate fruit. This is not to imply that we do not want to make a bona fide attempt at getting an appointment with our current prospect, but rather to suggest that we don't want to spend undue effort in doing so. When you really think about it, if a prospect is not ready, willing, and able to buy now, there is very little you can do to change this situation. Therefore, you need to know this as soon as possible so that you can move on to those prospects with a need for your product or service and make your investments there.

COMMANDMENT 4:   Be prepared with a list of names before you call.

Again, the Great God of the Sale is always watching. Not being prepared with a list of names will force you to devote much, if not all, of your prospecting hour to finding the names you need. You will have been busy, you will feel as though you worked hard, but you will have made no calls. I recommend having at least a one-month supply of names on hand at all times. I have found trading for leads to be the most effective way to build a prospect database other than purchasing the names from a highly qualified source. Remember, all salespeople are in the same boat. We are all in need of leads in order to survive.

It has been said many times in the past that time is money. However, I'm not aware that the following statement has ever been made before, so we'll step out on a limb and say it here. Leads are money too! In fact, they're the lifeblood of your career and should be treated with due respect. In order to trade leads, find someone in a complementary business, who is likely to call upon the same types of prospects that you are, and trade.

In my case, I am in the computer training business. I trade leads most often with sales representatives from software publishers. We both seek to find technology decision makers and influencers in large corporations. Companies selling training, other than computer training, would also be good trade candidates for me.

A second recommendation that will probably surprise many of you is to consider trading lists with your competitors. Although this might sound surprising, there is no more qualified list around other than your own, so why not trade?

After you have gotten over the shock of this recommendation, please consider the facts. First, I have found that there are no secrets as to who the decision makers in a company are. If you can find them, so can your competitor. If this is the case, why not develop a qualified list as soon as possible? By trading lists with your competitor, you will have substantially increased your effectiveness. Of course, both you and your competitor could have found every decision maker in the marketplace by yourselves. But this takes time. Trading lists will allow you to accomplish your goal of covering the market quite a bit faster than had you attempted to do it yourself.

Second, if you are not doing a good job servicing your customers, your competitors will wean them from you over time. If you are doing the best you can to service your customers, you will have nothing to worry about by having your competitor call on your leads. Finally, if your competitor cannot convert a lead, why not give you the opportunity? This action will stimulate demand in the industry and give your competitor (or you if the tables are turned) a better shot next time around.

Earlier I stated that trading leads is possibly the best way to develop a qualified list other than through purchased lists. When I refer to purchased lists, I want to distinguish between the type of list you would buy for direct-mail purposes and the type you would buy for telephone prospecting. Lists purchased for direct-mail purposes will typically have better prospects than those that you could quickly garner from your local business publication, public library, or Chamber of Commerce. A direct-mail list will have names of prospects who have at least expressed an interest in your type of product or service, or a closely related product or service. In contrast, lists taken from local business publications and other similar sources may not have expressed any interest in what you are selling. Recall our earlier discussion about purchased information and free information. Lists taken from your local business publication have a nominal cost (they are essentially free) and, as a result, you must spend a great deal of your own time to survey the list and find those prospects who might have an interest in your wares.

However, there are typically lists that are even better than those used for direct-mail purposes. These are lists that are highly qualified by the seller, typically through phone interviews and other techniques. In other words, the seller of the list has spent a great deal of time finding exactly who might have a strong interest in your product or service. This is time that you would otherwise have to spend yourself, which is why the sellers of the list can charge a premium for the prospects they provide to you. These lists can often provide you with multiple decision makers per company location and multiple company locations. Some lists go as far as to provide you with information on your prospects' strategic direction in the industry. These are the purchased lists that will yield your greatest return on investment.

COMMANDMENT 5: **Work without interruption.**

I recommend that you not take calls and not entertain meetings during your prospecting time. Take full advantage of the prospecting learning curve. As with any repetitive task, the more often you repeat the task during a contiguous block of time, the better you become. Prospecting is no exception to the rule. Your second call will be better than your first, your third better than your second, and so on. In sports, this practice is called getting in the groove. You will find that your prospecting technique actually improves over the course of your prospecting hour.

COMMANDMENT 6: Consider prospecting during off-peak hours if conventional prospecting times don't work.

Conventional cold calling hours are between 9:00 A.M. and 5:00 P.M. Set aside one hour each day during this period to prospect. When conventional cold calling hours are not working for you, consider switching or supplementing your prospecting time by prospecting during off-peak hours. Some of your best work will be done between 8:00 A.M. and 9:00 A.M., between noon and 1:00 P.M., and between 5:00 P.M. and 6:30 P.M.

I have found that truly successful people, and truly successful salespeople, do not work from 9:00 to 5:00. Rather, these hours are what I believe allow you to break even. You must put in that extra effort in order to be successful. I am not suggesting that you become a workaholic. Rather, I would always prefer to see you work *smart* as opposed to *hard*. However, the 110 Percent Solution, as Mark McCormack, the chairman of International Management Group, calls it, must be part of the equation.

You will find decision makers, go-getters like yourself, often work off-peak hours. You will find that their secretaries, those that often separate you from the person you are trying to reach, may not work during these hours. Take full advantage of these unguarded moments. But also take heed. When you call, be prepared to talk. The idea of calling during off-peak hours works with an extremely high degree of effectiveness. I have seen too many occasions where the salesperson dialed the phone, reached the person she dialed, and was unable to speak—this, after months of trying to reach the decision maker during conventional hours.

In addition to increasing your cold calling effectiveness, cold calling at off-peak hours will earn you the respect of those you are trying to reach. To me, the most crucial element of a sale is not what happens prior to the sale, but what happens after the sale. Think about going out to buy a car. Would you prefer that the salesperson give you a box of candy prior to the sale to earn your business or would you prefer that he or she be there after the sale to support this very expensive purchase? I would prefer the latter. Calling prospects during unconventional calling hours sends a clear message to the prospect. It says that you are dedicated to your work, your company, and your product. It says that you are the type of person who is going to go that extra mile to see that your customers get the return on their investment that they anticipated when they made the purchase.

I would recommend calling during off-peak hours as a supplement to prospecting during conventional hours and as a fall-back position when conventional prospecting times are simply not effective for you.

Special tip for Commandment 6: I have found one minute in particular to be unusually fruitful. This is 11:59. I'm not certain why this time has been so good for me—perhaps it is psychological; perhaps it is because companies are in transition at this time. Nonetheless, save this secret for your best prospects as 11:59 will only present you with a maximum of 250 golden opportunities! Also, as long as you are already prospecting, don't put down the phone. Consider moving on and prospecting from noon to 1:00 P.M. It will pay big dividends, especially after you read Commandment 9.

COMMANDMENT 7:   Vary your call times.

We are all creatures of habit. So are your prospects. In all likelihood, they are attending the same meeting each Monday at 10:00 A.M. If you cannot get through at this time, learn from your lack of success and call this particular prospect at other times during the day or on other days. You'll be amazed at the results. If you are wondering just how you might track your calls, let alone your call times, read Commandment 8.

COMMANDMENT 8:   Be organized.

I use a computerized contact management system called ACT!. I strongly suggest that you use a computerized system as well.

The contact management system you choose should allow you to record a follow-up call three years from tomorrow with no more difficulty than it would be to record one for tomorrow.

Here lies another great secret of prospecting. If a prospect tells you to call back in three years, six months, ten days, and five hours because his contract expires with his existing vendor on that date, do it! Nothing should fall through the cracks. Further, and possibly more important, because you can record your follow-up activity in such great detail, there should be no emotion associated with a "NO." When a prospect tells you the time is not right, you can simply schedule him for follow-up at a later date. As they say in the computer industry, it's as easy as 1-2-3.

The advantages of a computerized system are many. First, if you follow the recommendations outlined in this book, you are going to make a large number of prospecting calls. If you are like me, you may not remember the nature of every callback you get. You might be asking yourself, "Who is this person and why is she calling me?" If she is in your prospecting database, you will have your answer. She is returning your call. A computerized system gives you the ability to easily access your contact records.

Second, a computerized system allows you to keep detailed records on each of your prospects. In addition to the basics of name, address, and phone number, you can keep detailed records of call activity, call times, and even detailed call information. This information facilitates not only your initial call but also call follow-ups by making it quite easy to generate correspondence and mailings.

While I know that people were selling long before there were computers, computers certainly facilitate the sales and prospecting process. However, the key here is to be organized whether or not you use a computer system. Remember, the one who keeps the best notes wins.

COMMANDMENT 9:   See the end before you begin.

Stephen Covey, in his book *The Seven Habits of Highly Effective People*, tells us to see the end before we begin. Dr. Covey is, in effect, telling us to establish a goal and then develop a plan to work toward that goal. This sage advice works well in prospecting and business development. Your goal is to get the appointment, and your plan—your cold call script—should be designed to achieve your goal.

Dr. Covey's recommendation, coupled with a healthy dose of confidence, will do much to enhance your chances of making a successful cold call. I recommend that you use visualization techniques to enhance your level of confidence. Prospecting is fraught with rejection and sometimes even less than polite prospects. Much of this book, so far, has been devoted to teaching you how to overcome the anxiety associated with these negative influences. We now introduce one more idea to help you overcome the anxiety associated with rejection: confidence. Confidence will go a long way in overcoming the fear of rejection.

Before you begin each call, see the prospect eagerly awaiting your call and desperately in need of your services. You call to introduce yourself and the prospect responds, "Where have you been all my life!" You schedule the appointment. In other words, see your success before you make each call to ensure that both your confidence and enthusiasm are at peak levels.

This approach will have two major benefits. First, it will help move you toward Rejection-Proof Prospecting, a goal that we set earlier in this book. Remember, we should all believe that our product or service will make the customer better off. Your role is simply to spread the good word about your offering. Confidence will enhance your ability to do so and will allow you to make more calls.

Second, your confidence and enthusiasm will be contagious. After all, if you were the person on the other end of the phone, who would you be more likely to buy from: someone who is confident and feels strongly about his product or service or someone who is unsure of himself? I believe the answer is obvious.

COMMANDMENT 10:   Don't stop.

Persistence is one of the key virtues in selling success. I teach a seminar in Value-Added Selling for the American Management

Association. In that seminar, one topic that is covered is the Six Structures of Value Added. The Six Structures of Value Added are simply the ways or categories in which you can add value for your prospective customer during the sales cycle. The Six Structures of Value Added are information, distribution, resources, systems integration, stability, and product or service design. One of the six ways to add value to your product is through the stability of your organization. In other words, if you are buying a complex (and expensive) product or service from an organization, is it of value to you that the organization survive for the life of the product in order to honor its warranty and service the equipment? The answer is again an obvious "YES."

Customers value not only stability in the organization, but also stability in the salesperson. The salesperson must be available after the sale to support the product or service. It is the salesperson, hand in hand with the customer, who develops the value-added recommendations that help the customer enhance his or her profitability. There is a great deal of teamwork involved in an effort to optimize the value of your product in the client's organization. Further, if not for the expertise of the salesperson, it is not clear that the value-added strategies and recommendations will come to full fruition. Customers want to know that you will be there to help them implement the recommendations that you made.

The challenge is that you must have a way to demonstrate stability prior to a sale. The answer lies in persistence. Although I do not recommend calling a particular prospect once a day, I do strongly recommend following the call and visit goals outlined in Chapter 5. We discussed setting call goals of, say, once per month, for high-priority accounts. This plan should be tempered with a subjective assessment of the next appropriate time to call back. For example, if the prospect is on the verge of making a major decision, I would clearly call back more frequently. On the other hand, if the prospect has just signed a major two-year contract with one of your competitors, you may want to consider calling back less frequently. The key here is that you must call back. You can never lose a sale until you decide to quit. If you are persistent, while constantly trying to earn the right to advance, you will notice a change of attitude among your customers and prospects. They will begin to admire your persistence. They will understand that you are a force in the industry and a player to be reckoned with. You will get the appointment.

I have often read that most sales are made after the fifth call and most salespeople quit after the first. In order to keep my persistence at its peak, I reflect upon a very powerful story that I once read about persistence. This story would be enough to keep even the most complacent of us motivated to make the next call. The story is "Three Feet from Gold," from Napoleon Hill's classic, *Think and Grow Rich*. Briefly, the story is as follows:

> There was a man who left home to search for a gold mine. He went into the hills and discovered a very rich vein of ore. He had the gold analyzed to confirm his discovery and, sure enough, he had unearthed one of the purest veins of gold ever discovered. The man returned home to tell his friends and relatives so that he could borrow the necessary funds to cultivate the mine. He raised the necessary capital and returned to the mine to cultivate his fortune.
>
> The gold began to flow as easily as water and soon the man had recouped approximately half of his original investment. Then, without warning, the vein ended. The man dug furiously, but could not recapture the vein. Finally, he gave up, sold the mine and mining equipment to a junk dealer for scrap, and returned home, broke and a failure.
>
> Before scrapping the equipment, the junk dealer decided to hire a mining expert to study the mine. The expert, upon a detailed survey of the land, revealed that the vein had not dried up but rather shifted three feet to the left due to a fault in the earth. He advised that if the junk dealer were to continue digging in the new direction, he would soon recapture the vein and become fabulously wealthy. The junk dealer acted on the advice of his mining expert, went on to retap the vein of ore, and became one of the richest people in the United States. Meanwhile, the original miner had to live the remainder of his

days with the knowledge that he stopped "just three feet short of the gold."

How would you like to live with a similar feeling? Your next call, whether it be the fifth one to the same person over time or the thirtieth call of the day, could be the one that recaptures your vein of ore. Do you want to take the chance that you'll stop and someone else will collect the gold that really should have been yours? I certainly don't! Also, remember that most sales take place after the fifth call. Most salespeople stop after the first. Your persistence will pay off. It has to. This is the Law of Sowing and Reaping.

I would like to share an idea that has worked extremely well for me as a supplement to my persistence. Salespeople should have their own personal stationery for use with customers and prospects. Handwritten, hand-addressed, and hand-stamped notes and envelopes can do much to enhance the probability of success in the sales cycle by differentiating both you and your company as well as by demonstrating stability. While reading an industry publication or a general business publication, always be on the watch for information and articles about your customers and prospects. When you find a positive article, clip it out and send it to your customer, along with a congratulatory handwritten note. This practice will raise your visibility among your customers and prospects.

A Reminder

To reiterate, the Ten Commandments are:

Commandment 1:	Make an appointment with yourself for one hour each day to prospect.
Commandment 2:	Make as many calls as possible.
Commandment 3:	Make your calls brief.
Commandment 4:	Be prepared with a list of names before you call.
Commandment 5:	Work without interruption.
Commandment 6:	Consider prospecting during off-

	peak hours if conventional prospecting times don't work.
Commandment 7:	Vary your call times.
Commandment 8:	Be organized.
Commandment 9:	See the end before you begin.
Commandment 10:	Don't stop.

7

Anatomy of
a Cold Call

When I review the Ten Commandments of Prospecting, one thing becomes readily apparent: we need an eleventh commandment! The eleventh commandment should be practice, practice, and practice some more. Harvey Mackay, the noted author and public speaker, has an interesting saying: "Practice does not make perfect; perfect practice makes perfect." Whether practice or perfect practice makes perfect, one thing is very clear. In order to be effective at prospecting, you must practice.

All professionals practice. Skaters practice for years before a performance in the Olympics. Professional athletes practice day in and day out for their actual performances on the athletic field. Why should professional salespeople be any different? The question is practice what? I would recommend that you practice your cold calls. After all, does it make sense to learn on the job? Your reputation and success are at stake.

The first step in practicing your cold calls is to develop a script. The value of a cold calling script is several-fold. First, a script will ensure that you are prepared. In addition to the professional considerations of being prepared, being prepared will allow you to be in control of the call. If you are in control of the call, you will be much more at ease, since you will control the flow and direction of the conversation.

The second benefit of being prepared is consistency. Once you develop something that works, stick with it. A script will allow you to do that. I don't mean to imply that, once written, you should never again reevaluate your script. What I do mean to say is that there are core elements to a script. This chapter will teach you what they are. Although you should stick with the script that works for you, like a public speaker, always reevaluate your script to make it better. Never make major modifications to your script. Introduce small changes to your script, when appropriate, and test your changes in low-exposure environments.

I know that all of us have received cold calls both in the office and at home during the evenings. The calls can come from a variety of sources. The common thread of many of these calls is that it is clear the person on the other end of the phone is reading from a script. This type of cold call has done little to enhance the image of the professional salesperson. Believe it or not, the only thing that separates these types of calls from the truly professional calls is a little bit of practice.

I am a member of Toastmasters International. It is in my local Toastmasters Club that I have heard some of the best speeches of my life. I always ask the speakers the key to their success. Without exception, they all say practice. The typical Toastmaster will practice more than one month to deliver a speech of five to seven minutes. Investments in your script will help you become proficient, conversational, and relaxed. These skills will certainly increase your probability of success in the selling process.

I would venture to say that if I made 10,000 cold calls, each call would be identical in both form and substance. This may sound like quite a statement, but it's really not. I have dissected my cold call, put it back together, practiced it thousands of times, and fine-tuned it over numerous years of experience. An experienced veteran of corporate sales in our organization claims to make the same call each and every time she sits down to prospect.

I would like to present you with my cold calling script and then analyze its basic elements so that you can develop one of your own. Please notice that I am not asking you to use my script or the one used successfully by our sales veterans for more than forty years. Rather, I am asking you to learn from what we have done and then develop a script that suits your personality.

It would be very difficult for you to take a script that suits my nature and present it as naturally as I do. Rather, you must develop one that works for you, using the basic elements of a cold call as your guiding light. My prospecting script is presented in Figure 7-1.

I have studied public speaking for a number of years now and one of the greatest assets of a speaker is to sound conversational. This is very difficult to achieve and devastating to those speakers who cannot achieve it. The same could be said of prospecting with equal emphasis. Your cold call script must sound conversational in order to be effective. We have all received calls from someone who is obviously reading from a script. I'm sure we all have had the same reaction—to get off the phone as quickly as possible. Only a simple script can be conversational.

Let's take a few moments to analyze the elements of my script. While the words will change from person to person, the elements should remain constant. Once you find the perfect script for you, you'll never change and you'll never look back!

Get the Prospect's Attention

The first element of a successful cold call script is to get the attention of the prospect. Remember, he was not waiting for your call and was probably thinking about another subject when you called. Your first job is to break the prospect's preoccupation with what he was doing so that he pays attention to you. You have about ten seconds to accomplish this goal.

Figure 7-1. Basic cold calling script.

Mr. Jones please. Hello Mr. Jones. This is Paul Goldner of Sampson Management Company. How are you today? Great! The reason I'm calling is because I sent you some information about our organization in the mail. We provide financial management services to large organizations like yours. How do you handle your needs for those types of services at your company? (Mr. Jones responds.) Great! I'm going to be in your area on June 25 and would like to stop by and introduce myself. Are you available at 3:00?

The easiest way to get someone's attention is to state his or her name. Dale Carnegie, in his best-selling book *How to Win Friends and Influence People,* states that "A person's name is to that person the sweetest and most important sound in any language." Further, current studies indicate that people think about themselves 95 percent of the time. So, to get the prospect's attention, I use the following statement:

> Mr. Jones please. Hello Mr. Jones.

Not leaving anything to chance, I use the person's name twice in my opening statement. Further, please feel free to use the person's first name if this feels better for you. When people ask for Mr. Goldner, my first instinct is to look for my father.

Introduce Yourself

The second element of a successful cold call script is to introduce yourself. You should be quite accomplished with this and can consider the following statement:

> This is Paul Goldner of Sampson Management Company. How are you today? Great!

Introducing yourself is an integral part of the foregoing statement. However, what really makes the statement work is the phrase "How are you today?" Remember, you are making a cold call and the prospect knows this. There is a natural barrier between the prospect and yourself. What you need at this point is what professional speakers call an "ice breaker"—a phrase or statement delivered by the speaker to draw the audience into the speech. In this case, the ice breaker is designed to draw the prospect into your conversation. The phrase "How are you today?" works just great here. Interestingly enough, I almost never get a negative response to the question "How are you today?" The typical response I receive is either positive or neutral, at worst. This question also borrows from another of Dale Carnegie's strategies, to "[become] a good listener. [He] encourages others to talk about themselves." This advice is not only great for cold calling, but also for face-to-face selling. Obviously, it is also a key element in interpersonal relations.

Once I listen to the prospect's response, I always respond with an emphatic "Great!" *Great* is one of my favorite words. It has been said that selling is the transfer of enthusiasm about your product or service to the prospect. Once prospects become as enthusiastic about your offer as you are, you have made a sale. I start the transfer of enthusiasm from the point of first contact with the prospect. "Great" starts the transfer process.

There is a second key element built into this aspect of our cold call script. The "old school" of selling taught the salesperson to be a great presenter. The "new school" of selling teaches the salesperson to be a consultant. An effective consultant must listen to and understand the prospect's or customer's need. This requires the ability to ask effective questions. I like to start the consultative sales process during the cold call by asking two questions in my script. The first question is "How are you today?" As noted above, this question, albeit a simple one, establishes the framework for the consultative sales process.

State Your Reason for Calling

This is the third element in a successful cold call script. Consider this statement:

> The reason I'm calling is because I sent you some information about our organization in the mail. We provide financial management services to large organizations like yours.

Please note that although I state that the reason I called is because I sent Mr. Jones something in the mail, mail is not a required precursor to your cold call. Mail should be sent as part of a structured process or program. If it is not part of a process or program, it may serve to lengthen the sales cycle. Unfortunately, most salespeople send mail in order to avoid making the cold call. They believe that the prospect will read the mail and call in to place an order, removing the need for the cold call in the first place. As we noted earlier, this is not likely to be the case. The most likely outcome, that the prospect will not call, is not one that enhances the probability of a positive outcome in the sales process. In fact, you are likely going to be in exactly the same position with a given prospect if you send information prior to the cold call or if you don't. Thus, in order to speed up the process, I recommend that mail not be a prerequisite to the cold call process and that you should critically evaluate each and every piece of mail that you send out. You may receive a higher return on your investment by simply making more calls.

Please also note that I'm not recommending that you lie to your prospects. You are telling them that the reason you called is because you sent them something in the mail. Mail should be sent to support your cold calling efforts, not in place of them. Since it is unlikely that you will have made contact on your first call, you will have sent them a number of pieces of mail to support your prior calling effort. The important point is that the mail not be sent as a precursor to the call, but rather as a follow-up to the call.

I then continue by briefly telling Mr. Jones what we do. This is important because the prospects, whether they received the information or not, will likely require a synopsis of what you do. This also establishes the framework for the next and most crucial element of the cold call. In one sentence, I summarize the contents of our corporate literature. Using the basic cold calling script as an example, I might say, "We provide financial management services to large organizations like yours."

Ask a Question

Now that the prospect knows what you do, I put the ball back in his court by asking my second question. Consultative salespeople are at their best when they are asking probing, open-ended questions. The salesperson does very little talking and a lot of listening. By asking the following open-ended question, I give the prospect a great deal of latitude in telling me about his business and its needs. The big benefit to me is that because of the latitude I have given the prospect, he will, in all likelihood, give me the opportunity to identify a need of his company and thus establish the basis for a face-to-face appointment.

I ask:

How do you handle your needs for those types of services at your company?

Most telemarketing books that I have read recommend that you make a strong benefits statement at this point. A statement like the following would often be suggested:

Mr. Jones, I'm sure that you, like many of my best customers, would like to save several thousand dollars on the cost of . . .

To me, this approach is too manipulative. I'm not aware of anyone who would not like to save several thousand dollars. It's a silly question and the prospect might be offended that you asked it. Further, it is my strong belief that people will buy from you if you offer them an appropriate return on their investment. You can only do this if you first understand their business and their needs. Ultimately, the prospects must draw their own conclusion that they want to meet with you or buy your product or service. Your job is simply to help them along to reach this conclusion.

Listen carefully, and without interruption, to their response.

Get the Appointment

Now we go for the close. We have just listened attentively to how the prospect currently handles his need for our product or service. Then begin the transfer of additional enthusiasm and get the appointment.

Great! [Please note that your response of "Great" is in reference to the prospect's comments about how he

currently handles the need for your product or service
at his company. Again, the main reason that this word
is included in my cold call script is to build enthusiasm for your product and to sound confident in your
position as a valuable resource for the prospect.] I'm
going to be in your area on June 25 and would like
to stop by and introduce myself. Are you available at
3:00?

There are several important points here. First, before each
call, decide when it will be most convenient for you to meet
with the prospect. My schedule is always set up to maximize my
productivity, not the prospect's. Although this philosophy may
sound like it doesn't serve the needs of the prospect, remember
that the name of the game is to maximize your return on the
time you invest in the sales process. You should be flexible but
still keep in mind that you need to be as efficient as possible.

I recommend having an exact date and time to offer prospects. This date and time should be selected prior to your phone
call and should be the one that best suits your busy schedule. I
find that offering prospects only one time changes the focus of
the discussion to when they will meet with you. Offering alternative times, as recommended in other prospecting texts, leads
the discussion to if they will meet with you, not when. Remember, it is crucial that you get the appointment. By selecting Smart
Prospecting as your priority-setting mechanism, every appointment that you get is a good one, because every prospect lies
clearly within your target market.

A good schedule of appointments would be a meeting at
8:00 A.M. and then every two hours thereafter. Over the years, I
have found that a one-hour appointment is a good, solid meeting
and you can typically get from one end of any city in the country
to the other in the additional hour with time to spare. Your administrative duties such as letter writing, proposal writing, and
updating your database should be handled early in the morning,
late in the evening, and on the weekends. Your prospecting and
selling time is unfortunately limited to conventional business
hours. In most businesses, you can't see a prospect on a Sunday
afternoon or call one at 9:00 P.M. Because prospecting and selling

time are limited by conventions outside of your control, I recommend maximizing your prospecting efforts during the time allotted.

Review the Cold Call Script

A summary of the key elements of a cold call script follows:

1. Get the prospect's attention.
2. Introduce yourself.
3. State your reason for calling.
4. Ask a question.
5. Get the appointment.

Your job is to build a simple, conversational script that best reflects your sales personality.

Now that we understand the fundamental elements of a cold call script, it may be a good time to acknowledge that you don't always get the appointment. Therefore, we need a cold call and business development process or strategy that will ensure you will get sufficient appointments to satisfy your sales goals and increase your market penetration. This strategy is the subject of our next chapter. However, before moving on, I would like to introduce your Cold Calling Tool Kit: a collection of items that you should have with you when you do your prospecting. These items are all designed to give you that extra competitive edge that we first discussed in Chapter 1.

Your Cold Calling Tool Kit

Some of the items in your Cold Calling Tool Kit may appear a little unusual at first. In fact, when I review the kit at my seminars, I always hear people whispering the same question: "I wonder if he really does that stuff?" Well, the answer is "Yes I do!" and so will you once you see how helpful these suggestions will be.

The first element in your Cold Calling Tool Kit is a *mirror*.

Yes, a mirror. When making a cold call, it is imperative that you sound as good as you can over the telephone. The importance of how you sound on the phone cannot be overemphasized. You have exactly two minutes to convince a complete stranger to make an appointment with you. Even worse, the second you begin to speak, your prospects immediately begin to form a mental image of what they think about you. What do you want their mental image to be? It's up to you and the mirror will help. You should place your mirror directly in front of you, make certain that your hair is well groomed, that your clothes are neat and orderly, and that you sit up straight in your chair. This appearance check will make you sound powerful over the phone and help you to project confidence and conviction. When prospecting, you should never undo your tie, roll up your sleeves, slump in your chair, or put your feet up on the desk. All of these items will lessen the quality of your verbal image on the phone. I have a tendency to slump in my chair when I'm tired. One look in the mirror picks me right up. I continue with my calls and, more importantly, I project an image of power, confidence, and conviction.

I'm sure that you always try to look your best in your face-to-face selling opportunities. You would never dream of attending a business meeting looking disheveled because your appearance would likely disqualify you from the sales competition. Likewise, you should never sound disheveled over the phone. I have seen many salespeople over the years who look impeccable in person but sound disheveled over the phone. This greatly limits their opportunities in the sales world.

For those of you who might feel self-conscious with a mirror on your desk, I have found one for my desk that looks like a picture frame. From my side of the desk, it is a mirror. From the other side of the desk, it looks like the back of a picture frame. I have even had people turn it around asking to see my family.

The second tool in the kit is a *tape recorder*. For under $100, you can have a tape recorder hooked up to your telephone handset. Taping yourself allows you to answer the question, "If I were a prospect, would I give myself an appointment?" You may find the answer to this question very difficult to confront at first. However, it is important to know how we look and sound to others if we are to project the best possible sales image. When we speak, we hear ourselves through the vibrations of the bones in our head. When we listen to ourselves on a tape recorder, we hear ourselves as others do, through our ears. The difference is profound. Further, we all have little speech idiosyncrasies that we could do without. The most common of these are the *ah*'s and *um*'s that we use to fill up the time between thoughts and sentences. They can be very distracting and should be eliminated from your speech patterns. I am a member of Toastmasters International, a public speaking club that I would recommend to anyone who wants to improve their communication skills. At each Toastmasters meeting one designated club member counts the *ah*'s and *um*'s in the speeches—a very effective technique for eliminating these useless space fillers.

We all know how funny we look and sound to ourselves when we see ourselves on TV or hear ourselves on tape. All of us have much room for improvement. Your tape recorder will be a nice addition to your personal development program.

A third tool is a *telephone headset*. Telephone headsets are also a relatively inexpensive addition to your existing phone system. The headset frees your hands for taking orders, working on a computer, taking notes, and dialing the phone faster. All professional telemarketing groups make use of these devices. Further, headsets give you freedom to move about your office. It is not uncommon to have the prospect ask a question that requires you to look up the answer in a book. With a headset, you can continue the conversation, walk over to your bookshelf, and retrieve the information you are looking for without having the prospect know that you even moved.

A second benefit of a headset is that it allows you to stand when you speak on the phone. If you have ever watched a really great public speaker you will notice that the speaker was probably standing, not sitting. There are several reasons for this. The obvious one is that the speaker needs to be seen. The less obvious one is that the speaker can be more animated in a standing position. She can better use hand gestures and project her voice while standing. If selling success is in any way defined by the transfer of enthusiasm about your product or service from you to the prospect, then telephone headsets will give you much

greater freedom to stand as you prospect and project enthusiasm for your product or service with great emotion.

Fourth, consider the use of a *call timing device*, especially if
you have a tendency to make your prospecting calls last more
than two to three minutes. You do not need anything elaborate
to time your calls. A three-minute hourglass will tell you if you
are spending too much time on your prospecting calls. Remember, the purpose of your call is to get an appointment. Two to
three minutes should be sufficient in most instances to allow
you to accomplish your goal.

Fifth, never forget your trusty *script*. While I'm certain that
you will have internalized your script, and using it will be as
natural as speaking your own name, it pays to have it around in
the heat of battle. Sometimes, even the best of us lose our train
of thought, particularly when working during very stressful periods or if you don't have a private office. A handy script will
allow you to quickly collect your thoughts and resume the pur-
suit of your goal: the appointment.

8

Your Prospecting and Business Development Strategy

Before laying out our prospecting and business development strategy, it is important to understand the foundation upon which it is developed. The strategy we are about to unveil is based on three fundamental premises: the Law of Sowing and Reaping (Chapter 2), the Selling Life-Cycle Paradigm (Chapter 4), and consultative selling, in that you will always be providing your prospects with new and valuable information. In addition to these fundamental laws of professional selling, you must also understand that there are really only three potential outcomes to any given call: either you speak to the person you were trying to reach and get the appointment, you speak to the person you were trying to reach and don't get the appointment, or you don't reach the person you are targeting. These outcomes are presented graphically in Figure 8-1.

Getting the Appointment

Clearly, the first possibility—speaking to the person you were trying to reach and getting the appointment—is the easiest and most preferred outcome. Your basic script, detailed in the prior chapter, will work quite well here. In summary, you reach the person you were targeting and get the appointment. In this instance, a confirmation letter on the day you make the appointment would be a nice supplement to your call and calling a day in advance to confirm the appointment would also be a good

Figure 8-1. The three potential outcomes of a cold call.

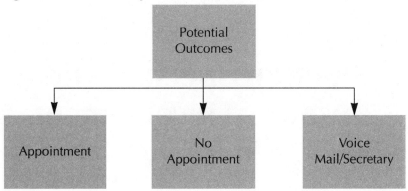

idea. A sample confirmation letter has been included in Figure 8-2 for your reference.

Sending a confirmation letter is extremely professional and will do a lot to enhance your position in the eyes of the prospect; so will calling a day in advance to confirm the appointment. This latter point is a hotly debated topic in the world of professional selling. Your options are to not call to confirm, to call a day in advance to confirm, as I recommend, or to call the day of the appointment to confirm. Those supporting the first position—not calling to confirm—argue that the prospect is then given an opportunity to cancel the appointment. Although this is true, I think the prospect has that option anyway by simply not being available when you arrive for the appointment. The prospect can either call you to cancel or may simply not be available when you arrive. Therefore, I suggest calling to confirm either the day before the appointment or the day of the appointment. Either option works. If you call a day in advance and the prospect cancels the appointment, you have more time to react and salvage the hour or two that you planned for the meeting. Canceled appointments give you a great opportunity to do additional prospecting.

Losing a Sale: What Next?

This first part of our business development strategy is depicted in Figure 8-3. In summary, you call the person you were target-

Figure 8-2. Sample confirmation letter.

June 2, 19XX

Mr. Robert Jones
Director of Administration
NYT International
15 South Salem Avenue
Lower Newton Falls, MA 06000

Dear Mr. Jones:

It was a pleasure to speak with you yesterday. I look forward to our meeting on Wednesday, June 25, 19XX at 10:00. I will call the day before to confirm the appointment. In the interim, should you require any information or if I can be of assistance, please do not hesitate to call.

Yours very truly,

Susan Simms
Account Manager

---

ing and get an appointment. You use your basic script to do this. Once you get the appointment, you send a confirmation letter (Figure 8-2). You also call one day in advance of your appointment to confirm. Ultimately, you will go on a meeting, develop a proposal for the prospect, and either win or lose a sale. Assuming that you win, your job is to provide superior customer service. However, what do you do if you lose the sale? This is where most salespeople stop the business development process. We are just beginning.

Figure 8-3. Business Development Strategy—Part One.

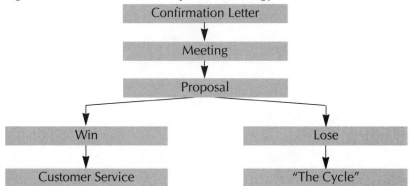

If you reflect back to Smart Prospecting, we went to great lengths to define our target market. Our definition was based on one or more objective demographic factors. Losing a sale does not change the demographics of the prospect account. Even though we lost the sale, we must place the prospect back in our sales pipeline and continue to work with him in some manner. This is exactly the point we were making when we first introduced you to the Selling Life-Cycle Paradigm. A "NO" today simply means that you place the prospect back into the sales pipeline for continued cultivation. The question that comes to mind is, What do you do to further cultivate the account? After all, you just lost a sale!

After losing a sale, I recommend that you place your prospect into the "Business Development Cycle" (Figure 8-4). The Business Development Cycle may be one of the most powerful tools we have available as professional salespeople. We will use this tool to recultivate lost sales, to overcome objections, and even to overcome voice mail. The cornerstone of the Business Development Cycle is your company's unique selling points.

Over the years, I have taught thousands of professionals how to sell. One interesting observation that I have made during this time is that every company has its strengths relative to the competition. The key to making the Business Development Cycle work for you is to have a good command of your com-

Figure 8-4. The business development cycle.

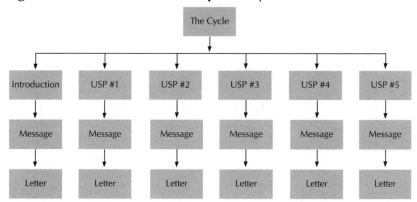

pany's strengths or unique selling points. In order to illustrate how the Business Development Cycle works, let us assume that you work for Office Tech, Incorporated. Office Tech is a global organization that manufactures high-technology office equipment. The unique selling points and the related customer benefits are outlined as follows:

[First-to-market commitment] Office Tech is consistently first to market with new products. This allows Office Tech customers to stay on the cutting edge of technology.

[Local field service support] Because Office Tech is a global organization, it provides its customers with local field service support for all installed units. The big benefit to Office Tech customers is minimized downtime for all installed applications.

[Global organization] As noted above, Office Tech is a global organization. The company is able to support other multinational corporations as well as to provide local support for all installed equipment sold.

[Broad product line] Office Tech sports the broadest product line in the industry, providing high-technology office equipment along all lines of the price/performance spectrum. Office Tech serves as a single-source solution to its customers.

[Research and development testing facility] Office Tech not only supports the largest research and development budget in the industry, but also allows customers and prospects to test potential applications of Office Tech products in its own testing facility without charge to the customer.

I encourage you to spend a few moments outlining your company's unique selling points. Figure 8-5 has been provided for your convenience. Your unique selling points are going to be critical factors in your selling success and will be used throughout the remainder of this book. Accordingly, you should become intimately familiar with them. In fact, you should be able to recite them in your sleep and they should permeate each and every sales conversation and presentation that you make.

Figure 8-5. Sample form for compiling your company's unique selling points.

Unique Selling Points
for

_____

Office Tech Incorporated	Your Company
Global Organization	
First to Market Commitment	
Local Field Service Support	
Broad Product Line	
R&D Testing Facility	

The Business Development Cycle allows you to continue to work with a prospect, even though you just lost a sale. The reason is, each time you call the prospect, you are providing her with new information. In other words, you are giving the prospect a new reason to call you back, a new reason to meet with you, and a new reason to buy. Second, you are prepared each and every time that you call. Let's see how to use the Business Development Cycle to overcome your lost sale.

Assume that you just lost a sale to a priority one account. Based on the parameters we outlined in the Smart Prospecting chapter you would be required to call the prospect once a month, even after the lost sale. The issue becomes, then, what should you say? Here's where your unique selling points come in. The reason that you may have lost the sale is because you may not have been as effective as necessary in tying the needs of your prospect back to one or more of your strengths or unique selling points. If you recall, we had defined selling as an education process and here is where the education begins. What we are going to do is develop a series of scripts around each of our unique selling points. In this way, you will always have something new and interesting to present to your prospects. In other words, you will be giving them a new reason to return your call if you are facing voice mail, a new reason to meet with you if you are having difficulty getting an appointment, and a new reason to buy if you are not making a sale. Assuming that you just lost a sale, the next time you speak with a prospect, you may want to have your message focus on the first of your five unique selling points. A sample script, using the first of the unique selling points of Office Tech, is outlined in Figure 8-6. Assuming that you get the appointment, your standard confirmation letter will work just fine (Figure 8-2). However, assuming that you don't get the appointment, a follow-up letter, reaffirming your first-to-market commitment, would be very appropriate. A sample follow-up letter has been provided in Figure 8-7.

Again, assuming that you didn't get the appointment by using your first-to-market strategy, you would be required to call the prospect in another month. This time, however, you would focus on local field service support instead of the first-to-market commitment. A sample script and follow-up letter have

Figure 8-6. Sample script for a call focusing on your first unique selling point.

Mr. Jones please. Hello Mr. Jones. This is Susan Simms of Office Tech. How are you today? Great! The reason I'm calling is because we were recently FIRST TO MARKET with a new piece of high-technology office equipment that will revolutionize the way companies do business. We have success-fully installed this machine at a number of organizations like yours and I would like to come by and demonstrate it to you. I'm going to be in your area on September 27 and would like to stop by. Are you available at 3:00?

been provided for your reference in Figures 8-8 and 8-9, respec-tively. Assuming that you do not get the appointment this time, you move on to your third unique selling point, then your fourth, and then your fifth. Sample scripts and follow-up letters have been provided in Figures 8-10 through 8-15.

The strategy we are outlining here teaches you an effective way to penetrate accounts. Many salespeople enter a new selling situation expecting to become the exclusive provider of goods or services for the target company immediately. This is akin to say-ing to the prospect: "Hello. You don't know me. Would you please give me all of your business?" If someone were to ask this question of you, how would you react? Let's review this strategy by taking a look at Figure 8-16.

I would like to suggest that all prospects have two types of business: core business and niche business. Core business is defined as a prospect's main opportunity. It is currently the largest piece of the pie and the target that all salespeople typi-cally aim for. Niche business, on the other hand, is a business opportunity that is either not readily identified or not readily serviced. If the niche opportunity is not readily identified, the prospect is typically unaware of the need and, most often, it can only be revealed through skillful questioning on the part of the salesperson. In the case where the niche opportunity is not readily serviced, the prospect is aware of the need, but has yet to find a qualified source of supply.

The problem with setting your sights on only the core busi-

Figure 8-7. Sample follow-up letter focusing on your first unique selling point.

September 15, 19XX

Mr. Robert Jones
Director of Administration
NYT International
15 South Salem Avenue
Lower Newton Falls, MA 06000

Dear Mr. Jones:

It was a pleasure to speak with you today. As you know, Office Tech recently introduced a new piece of high-technology office equipment that will revolutionize the way companies do business. The release of this new product demonstrates our continued commitment to be First to Market with new high-technology office products.

Given the size of your organization and your commitment to provide state-of-the-art products to your customers, I thought this new equipment might be of value to you. We are seeing a strong growth trend in this area among our largest corporate accounts.

I have enclosed some product literature for your review and will be contacting you shortly to discuss your interest in this program. In the interim, should you require additional information or have any questions, please do not hesitate to contact me.

Yours very truly,

Susan Simms
Account Manager

Figure 8-8. Sample script focusing on your second unique selling point.

Mr. Jones please. Hello Mr. Jones. This is Susan Simms of Office Tech. How are you today? Great! The reason I'm calling is to tell you about our new field service support program called Customer Care 100. Because we are a global organization, we have LOCAL FIELD SERVICE representatives in each city where you have offices. This ensures that we are able to provide on-site service to your remote locations within twenty-four hours, minimizing your downtime. We have been successful in saving organizations like yours many thousands of dollars through this program and I would like to come by and discuss it with you. I'm going to be in your area on April 19 and would like to stop by. Are you available at 3:00?

ness is that the prospect likely has already identified the need for what you do and has found a provider for the product or service. Further, if the current provider is not doing an adequate job, the prospect has likely replaced them with someone who will. In other words, it is unlikely for you to walk in off the street and get the core business. This may happen, but it's more likely the result of luck than a well-planned strategy.

As an alternative, I would like to suggest that you develop a strategy around niche opportunities. These niche opportunities should be based on your unique selling points. Keeping in mind that the prospects likely have fulfilled their needs for the core business opportunity, you must continuously search for new and innovative ways to help them achieve their goals. If you simply offer the "status quo," why should a prospect take time out of his or her already busy day to meet with you? Presenting new and innovative ways to improve a prospect's profitability will help you win those smaller sales that come from the prospect's niche opportunities and your unique selling points. This will give you the opportunity to prove your capabilities. Once you have done this, you can then move to additional smaller sales and ultimately larger sales. As you continue to earn the right to advance, you have also followed a tactical strategy that allows you to surround the core business opportunity. At this

Figure 8-9. Sample follow-up letter focusing on your second unique selling point.

April 5, 19XX

Mr. Robert Jones
Director of Administration
NYT International
15 South Salem Avenue
Lower Newton Falls, MA 06000

Dear Mr. Jones:

It was a pleasure to speak with you today. As you know, Office Tech recently introduced its new Customer Care 100 program. This program ensures twenty-four-hour on-site services in all of your locations world-wide.

Given the size of your organization and your need to minimize down-time for all office equipment, I thought this new program might be of value to you. We are seeing a strong need in this area among many of our largest corporate accounts.

I have enclosed some program literature for your review and will be contacting you shortly to discuss your interest in this program. In the interim, should you require additional information or have any questions, please do not hesitate to contact me.

Yours very truly,

Susan Simms
Account Manager

Figure 8-10. Sample script focusing on your third unique selling point.

Mr. Jones please. Hello Mr. Jones. This is Susan Simms of Office Tech. How are you today? Great! The reason I'm calling is to tell you about the new office we just opened in Bangkok. This increases the number of offices we support to 110 worldwide. By having in excess of a hundred locations worldwide, we are able to provide your remote locations with the same level of customer service and support that you now receive in the United States. Many of our customers now enjoy the benefits of working with a multinational office equipment supplier and I would like to introduce you to these same benefits. I'm going to be in your area on March 21 and would like to stop by. Are you available at 3:00?

---

point, it becomes appropriate to discuss exclusive providership with your customer.

The system can also be related to our recommendations in Chapter 5. If you remember, we recommended that you call your high-priority accounts once a month, your middle-priority accounts once a quarter, and your low-priority accounts once every half year. Following this type of a callback strategy and combining it with the unique selling point messages outlined in this chapter gives you a half year's worth of messages if you are calling a high-priority account, eighteen months worth of messages if you are calling a middle-priority account, and three years worth of messages if you are calling a low-priority account. In other words, you always have something new and important to say to your prospects.

Further, the system is recyclable. When you get to the end, you simply start over. You can start by reintroducing your company to the prospect. After all, quite a bit of time has passed since you lost the original sale. Further, when you get to your unique selling point messages, they will have a slightly different slant. In other words, you are delivering a series of new and improved messages. By employing this strategy, you will also be demonstrating perhaps the greatest quality or virtue of professional selling: persistence. After all, the prospect is going to

(text continues on page 78)

Figure 8-11. Sample follow-up letter focusing on your third unique selling point.

March 16, 19XX

Mr. Robert Jones
Director of Administration
NYT International
15 South Salem Avenue
Lower Newton Falls, MA 06000

Dear Mr. Jones:

It was a pleasure to speak with you today. As you know, Office Tech just celebrated the opening of its 110th office in Bangkok, Thailand. By expanding our worldwide network, we are able to provide better service and support to global organizations like yours.

Given the size of your organization and your need for local service and support, I thought this new office opening might be of interest to you. We are seeing a strong interest in our expansion among many of our largest corporate accounts.

I have enclosed some corporate literature for your review and will be contacting you shortly to discuss your interest in our organization. In the interim, should you require additional information or have any questions, please do not hesitate to contact me.

Yours very truly,

Susan Simms
Account Manager

Figure 8-12. Sample script focusing on your fourth unique selling point.

Mr. Jones please. Hello Mr. Jones. This is Susan Simms of Office Tech. How are you today? Great! The reason I'm calling is to tell you about two new models we just brought to market. Our first model, the XT100, allows users to expand their prior capacity levels by 100 percent. This model is the most sophisticated version of our XT product line. The second model, the XT50, is designed for new users of our products. It is quite a bit less expensive, yet lets new users enjoy many of the benefits of our more sophisticated versions. Office Tech is very proud of the COMPLETE SPECTRUM of products we bring to the market. This allows our customers to enjoy a single source of supply for all of their office equipment needs. I'm going to be in your area on January 17 and would like to stop by. Are you available at 3:00?

Figure 8-13. Sample follow-up letter focusing on your fourth unique selling point.

January 10, 19XX

Mr. Robert Jones
Director of Administration
NYT International
15 South Salem Avenue
Lower Newton Falls, MA 06000

Dear Mr. Jones:

It was a pleasure to speak with you today. As you know, Office Tech just brought two new products to market. Our first model, the XT100, allows users to expand their prior capacity levels by 100 percent. This model is the most sophisticated version of our XT product line. The second model, the XT50, is designed for new users of our products. It is quite a bit less expensive, yet lets new users enjoy many of the benefits of our more sophisticated versions. Office Tech is very proud of the complete spectrum of products we bring to the market. This allows our customers to enjoy a single source of supply for all of their office equipment needs.

I have enclosed some product literature for your review and will be contacting you shortly to discuss your interest in these new additions to the Office Tech family. In the interim, should you require additional information or have any questions, please do not hesitate to contact me.

Yours very truly,

Susan Simms
Account Manager

Figure 8-14. Sample script focusing on your fifth unique selling point.

Mr. Jones please. Hello Mr. Jones. This is Susan Simms of Office Tech. How are you today? Great! The reason I'm calling is to tell you about our new research and development testing facility. As you know, Office Tech supports the largest research and development budget in the industry. With our new facility, we are not only capable of supporting our own commitment to research and development but also can extend our commitment to our customers by allowing you to test applications in our laboratory, free of charge. Office Tech is very proud of its COMMITMENT TO RESEARCH AND DEVELOPMENT. This allows our customers to enjoy state-of-the-art technology and a first-to-market commitment across our complete product line. I'm going to be in your area on June 2 and would like to stop by. Are you available at 3:00?

Figure 8-15. Sample follow-up letter focusing on your fifth unique selling point.

May 15, 19XX

Mr. Robert Jones
Director of Administration
NYT International
15 South Salem Avenue
Lower Newton Falls, MA 06000

Dear Mr. Jones:

It was a pleasure to speak with you today. As you know, Office Tech just opened a new research and development testing facility. With our new facility, we are not only capable of supporting our own commitment to research and development but also can extend our commitment to our customers by allowing you to test applications in our laboratory, free of charge. Office Tech is very proud of its commitment to research and development. This allows our customers to enjoy state-of-the-art technology and a first-to-market commitment across our complete product line.

I have enclosed some literature about our new facility for your review and will be contacting you shortly to discuss your interest in this new addition to the Office Tech family. In the interim, should you require additional information or have any questions, please do not hesitate to contact me.

Yours very truly,

Susan Simms
Account Manager

Figure 8-16. "Core/Niche" diagram.

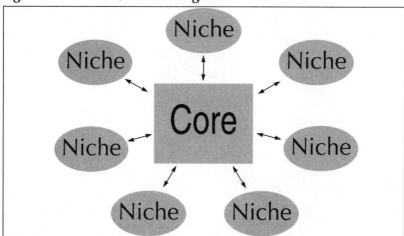

want to know that you will be there to follow up on the sale. Persistence sends a very clear message to the marketplace.

This chapter outlined a business development strategy that forms the foundation of our approach to prospecting. Thus far, we have covered the basic script, to be used when we reach a prospect and get an appointment. We have also covered what to do after you get an appointment, paying particular attention to the possibility that you may not win the sale, yet you still need to cultivate the prospect. Our next chapter explores handling objections.

9

Handling
Objections

Recently, I taught a prospecting seminar at a franchise organization. I had just completed the "Anatomy of a Cold Call" segment and someone from the Boston franchise raised her hand and said that all of this sounded fine to her, but in Boston, the calls don't always go as smoothly. Well, calls don't go that smoothly in New York, my hometown, either, or anywhere else in the country for that matter. The woman who asked the question was referring to the fact that her prospects don't always readily agree to meet with her. Rather, they provide her with reasons why they don't want to meet—that is, *objections.*

There are two interesting characteristics about objections. First, there are only a limited number of objections that you will come across in your selling career. This has tremendous implications! Since there are only a limited number of objections, we can plan for the objections and also plan our responses. Second, objections really aren't objections at all. They are simply a request by the prospect for additional information.

Assume that you are trying to set up a meeting with a particular prospect. Assume further that the prospect does not want to meet with you because of a particular reason. What the prospect is really telling you is that you have not provided him with enough information at this point to justify taking time out of his busy schedule to see you. There is some tremendous synergy here. Since we can plan for the objections and respond to them by providing additional information, we should be able to turn around any objection with the same skill and ease that our prospects send them our way.

I have compiled what I believe to be a comprehensive list of objections. There are only seven objections on this list. I also provide you with a well-developed response or two to each objection. Like the basic script, my responses should be used for guidance. Your response should be consistent with your industry and personality. Only then will you continue to sound conversational.

Developmental Stages in the Learning Process

Before we actually address objections, I would like to provide you with one additional insight. Adult learners go through four stages of development in the learning process: unconscious incompetence, conscious incompetence, conscious competence, and unconscious competence. In the first stage—unconscious incompetence—the adult learner, or salesperson in our case, is not aware of what he doesn't know. Essentially, the salesperson is a newcomer to a particular skill. During the second phase, the salesperson becomes aware of his lack of skills and is very concerned about the deficiency. In the third stage of development, the salesperson starts to become better at the particular skill set; however, he must constantly think about what he is doing in order to accomplish the task. Finally, he can perform the task extremely well, without thinking about it at all.

It is the unconscious competence stage that we are striving for in our cold calling efforts. Both our script and our planned responses to objections must be reflex on our part. The entire cold call process lasts only two to three minutes and you must be able to think and react quite rapidly during the entire call. The only way to reach this stage is to practice, practice, and practice. Yes, I did say practice. Why learn on your real live prospects? Once you get someone on the phone, you'll have one shot, the two to three minutes, to get the appointment. You wouldn't want to get off the phone knowing that you could have done much better. It may be a year before you'll have the opportunity to speak with the prospect again. I practice my prospecting script and responses in much the same way as I prepare for a speech. I go over the information again and again until I have it just right. Only then do I get on the phone and start dialing.

Famous Objections

The following is the list of objections that we plan to address:

Send me literature.

We handle the need for your product [service] internally.

We have an existing relationship.

I'm not the person responsible for this.

We do not have the budget for your product or service.

Your price is too high.

We have used your company in the past and were dissatisfied.

Send Me Literature

In my experience, this response is the most commonly used objection. You reach a prospect on the phone and he tells you to send some information in the mail. Most salespeople respond to this objection in a positive manner. They send the information as requested and believe that they have moved one step further in the sales cycle. My experience, however, has been that in most instances, you are no further along in the sales cycle than you were prior to the call. Once you hang up the phone, the prospect is going to return to whatever he was doing. He is not going to spend much time, if any, reflecting on the brief discussion you just had. When he receives the information several days later, he may remember your discussion, but in all likelihood he will not. It has been my experience that prospects use this objection to make the salesperson feel as though she has made a positive step in the sales cycle. The prospect can issue the objection without getting into a detailed discussion with the salesperson. This objection will also minimize the prospect's investment in the phone call.

Since this objection is extremely common, I have planned our response in our basic script. A prospect asking us to send literature prior to agreeing to a meeting has played right into our hands. Remember, we have already told the prospect the reason we are calling is to follow up on the information we *already* sent. My response is presented in Figure 9-1.

There are several interesting points here. First, the prospect can only respond in one of two ways. He can agree to meet with you or he can provide you with an additional (real) objection that we will address below. Second, notice I am asking the prospect if he will be available. I am not going to simply drop off the information. I could hire a messenger or send it through the mail if that is what I wanted to accomplish. I am going to have a meeting—and not a brief meeting either. Very rarely, if ever, will these "drop off the information meetings" last less than one hour. In fact, these meetings are in every way the same as the ones that were planned by the prospect. Finally, I always call to confirm.

We Handle the Need for Your Product [Service] Internally

This objection tends to be a very powerful one because it would appear to be difficult to overcome. After all, why would prospects buy from you if they already make what you are selling themselves? However, overcoming this objection should be no more difficult than any other. As always, the key lies in preparation. If you refer to our "Core/Niche" diagram, included in Fig-

Figure 9-1. Sample script responding to the "send me literature" objection.

Since I've already sent you information, it must have gotten lost in the mail. I'm going to be in your area on March 16. Why don't I stop by at 3:00 and drop it off. Will you be available? Great! I'm noting this in my planner and will call you the day before to confirm.

ure 9-2, what you should quickly come to realize is that by telling you the prospect company handles the need for your product or service internally, you are being told that the company has filled the core need for your product or service itself. Keep in mind that had the company not filled the need for your product or service itself, one or more of your competitors might have the business. Therefore, this objection and the following objection—the one in which the prospect tells you that he is happy with the services of one of your competitors—are very similar objections. The strategy for overcoming both objections will also be very similar. Further, we already established that most prospects will likely be aware of their need for your product and will have likely found a stable source of supply. Therefore, this objection should not come as a surprise at all. Rather, besides the first objection covered in this chapter, the internal and competitor objections are the two most frequently used by prospects. I suspect that the three objections combined account for the majority of all objections you will receive.

Interestingly enough, the internal objection can be handled in one of two ways. The way in which you handle the objection is a function of who in the prospect organization you are working with: middle managers or upper managers. Each response

Figure 9-2. "Core/Niche" diagram.

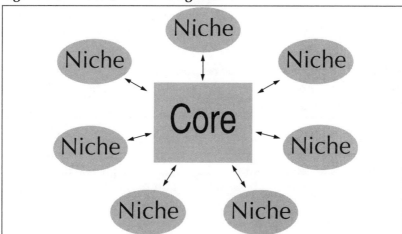

would be different because each classification of manager has a different set of interests or value system. Your response must be designed to reflect the interest of the party to whom you are talking.

Middle-Management Approach

An approach I like to recommend with regard to middle management is to address one of their primary concerns: efficiency. Whatever they are doing is fine; you should just position yourself to help them do it better. This can easily be accomplished if we refer to Figure 9-2. Here, middle management is typically proficient at addressing the core set of business needs. However, they will typically not have the capabilities, resources, or economies of scale to address, or cost effectively address, niche needs. All organizations have niche needs or opportunities and this should be the target of your comments. The approach of addressing niche opportunities will be very unthreatening to a middle-management prospect because you are offering help by acting as a supplement to their existing offering. You are not trying to take away their job by eliminating the need for what they do. My recommended response is presented in Figure 9-3.

After reviewing Figure 9-3, you might be wondering what you would do if the prospect asks you just how you can supplement his internal capabilities. This is where your unique selling points come in. In Chapter 8, we outlined our unique selling

Figure 9-3. Sample script for responding to the "we handle the need for your product [service] internally" objection—middle manager approach.

Great! That was exactly my reason for the call. We have worked with a number of large organizations like yours and have found that we can be an effective supplement to the services you already provide through your organization. I'm going to be in your area on August 5 and would like to stop by to show you how. Are you available at 3:00?

points and constructed a business development strategy around them. Any one of these unique selling points could serve as a supplement to the prospect's internal capabilities. For example, assume that you work for a company that sells plastic resins, and your prospect uses plastic resin in a variety of commercial and industrial applications. Assume further that the company was developing a new application and wanted to test the application in a laboratory prior to full-scale production. The options are to build a testing facility for internal use or to rent a facility each time a new application must be tested. You just happened to call and the prospect responds by giving you the internal objection. You reply with the script outlined in Figure 9-3. The company wants clarification on exactly how you can supplement its capabilities. Your answer is outlined in Figure 9-4. Although this method might sound too good to be true, it works. You are trying to identify niche opportunities to supplement your prospect's strong internal capabilities. Any of your unique selling points could provide compelling reasons to get together. I also recommend that you prepare a letter to send to the prospect to support your discussion. A sample letter has been provided for your reference in Figure 9-5.

Figure 9-4. Sample script for adding to your response to the "we handle the need for your product [service] internally" objection—middle manager approach.

Ms. Jansen, recently our company opened a new research and development testing facility to support our first-to-market commitment. Not only does this facility support our internal research and development efforts, but we have also allowed our customers the opportunity to use our facility to test potential applications prior to full-scale production. We have found that many organizations like yours view this as a major benefit of doing business with us and I thought it might be of value to you. I would like to stop by next Tuesday at 3:00 to introduce myself and share with you other areas in which we might be able to supplement your strong internal capabilities.

Figure 9-5. Sample follow-up letter for responding to the "we handle the need for your product [service] internally" objection—middle manager approach.

July 30, 19XX

Ms. Sally Jansen
Director of Manufacturing
International Plastic Company
45 Roberts Drive
Kansas City, MO 66631

Dear Ms. Jansen:

It was a pleasure to speak with you today. As we had discussed, we have worked with a number of large organizations like yours and have found that we can be an effective supplement to the services you already provide through your organization.

For example, recently our company opened a new research and development testing facility to support our first-to-market commitment. Not only does this facility support our internal research and development efforts, but we have also allowed our customers the opportunity to use our facility to test potential applications prior to full-scale production. We have found that many organizations like yours view this as a major benefit of doing business with us and I thought it might be of value to you. I would like to stop at your convenience to introduce myself and share with you other areas in which we might be able to supplement your strong internal capabilities.

I have enclosed some corporate literature for your review and will be contacting you shortly to reassess your interest in our company. In the interim, should you require additional information or have any questions, please do not hesitate to contact me.

Yours very truly,

Paul Robertson
Senior Account Executive

Upper-Management Approach

Middle management is typically concerned with doing a better job. This makes their life easier and also allows them to potentially progress to upper management. Our supplemental approach works well with middle management because it will help them achieve their goal of doing a better job. Upper management, on the other hand, is typically concerned with return on investment, earnings per share, and other broad-based financial performance ratios. Thus, your response to an upper-management internal objection should show them that you can increase the profitability of their company.

Before we craft our upper-management response, let us understand why we are so well positioned to increase the profitability of a prospect organization that handles the need for your product or service internally. First, economies of scale typically rest with you. Economies of scale say that you can produce the same product that they can but you can do it more cost effectively. If you can produce the product more cost effectively, then you are in a position to provide the prospects with a lower total cost solution. (If you are not well positioned to provide the prospects with a lower total cost solution, you can always use the middle-management supplementary response as your fallback position.) Hence, you can improve the profitability of their organization. Economies of scale typically rest with you because your organization is highly focused on the production of the product or service in question. Prospect organizations are in business to produce the product or service that they sell to their customers and the production of your product or service is not the main focus of their attention. Accordingly, it stands to reason that you should be more effective at the production of your product or service than they are.

In addition to economies of scale, your organization typically services a broader base or population of customers than their internal population for your product. Their organizations serve only their internal customer base while yours serves many organizations within your target market. You have a much larger base over which to amortize your research and development costs and spread your risks, so you can produce your products or services more cost effectively.

One of the greatest risks facing an organization today is the risk of technological obsolescence. Products, services, and systems are changing at an ever-increasing rate and an internal organization with a smaller customer base may not have the resources to justify a large investment in current technology. Your organization will. In other words, your organization will be a nice alternative when it comes to outsourcing the risk of technological obsolescence and outsourcing research and development efforts outside of the target company's core competencies.

It is important when working with upper management that you be prepared to speak their language. Upper management speaks primarily a financial language. You are preparing to tell them that you can provide them with a lower total cost solution than the one they have in place. I am certain that they will be interested in your response, but I am equally certain that they will want you to justify your position. The ability to quantify the impact of your recommendation is crucial to your success with upper management.

In training business, many companies in our target market often find themselves discussing the alternatives of outsourcing the administration for their training program or handling the registration function internally. Typically, the internal registration function can be managed by one individual at an annual salary of $25,000 to $35,000. Using the average, let us assume that the internal registrar is paid $30,000 per annum.

In order to fully understand the outsourcing alternative, you must understand that a person's salary is only one element of the total cost of keeping a person on the company payroll. In addition to the person's salary, there are added costs of benefits such as health care and vacation; overhead costs in that you must provide the person with a desk, a phone, other office equipment, and a place to work; management time since you want to provide the employee with an appropriate level of supervision; and inefficiencies since you can count on the employee getting sick and you having to pay a temporary employee for the day to replace the lost manpower.

These additional costs are known as a corporate burden rate. The corporate burden rate is designed to reflect the total cost of employment for an organization, not just the cost of the employee's salary. A corporate burden rate can range as low as 120 percent for many small companies to as high as 270 percent for many Fortune 2000 companies. I always like to use the approximate average in this range of 200 percent, or twice the employee's salary. Continuing with the analysis, the registrar now has an internal cost to the organization of $60,000, not the $30,000 first contemplated.

There is one other important distinction here. An employee is a fixed cost to an organization—that is, you pay for the resource irrespective of usage. Assuming that you fully utilize the resource (for the 250 working days in a year), the daily internal rate for registration services would be $240 per day ($60,000 divided by 250 days in a year). However, if you only use the resource to 75 percent of its efficiency, your daily rate rises to $320 per day. Although this figure might not seem significant at this point, a comparable rate for an outsourced event registration service might be $100 per day, or approximately 30–40 percent of your internal cost. The other big benefit in this analysis is that the outsourced resource is a strictly variable cost. In other words, you pay for it only when you use it.

This type of quantitative argument can be quite compelling and should be coupled with qualitative factors such as quality (we should be able to provide the service more effectively since this is our line of business), ease of administration (when employees call in sick, it is our responsibility to replace them, not yours), ease of recruitment (it is our responsibility to find qualified resources), and ease of doing business (the customer has one point of contact for all of her needs in a particular area). Having developed both the quantitative and qualitative elements of my analysis, I might respond to the internal objection as outlined in Figure 9-6 when working with upper management.

You begin with the trademark transfer of enthusiasm. The prospect has just told you that he doesn't need you because he can provide your product or service internally, and you are completely undaunted by his response. Further, the prospect is ex-

Figure 9-6. Sample script for responding to the "we handle the need for your product [service] internally" objection—upper management approach.

Great! That was exactly my reason for the call. We have worked with a number of large organizations like yours and have found outsourcing to be a lower total cost solution to their needs. I'm going to be in your area on July 18 and would like to stop by to show you why. Are you available at 3:00?

---

pecting you to be completely overwhelmed because he has just told you that he can do what you do by himself and you respond by saying that's exactly why you called. This leaves the prospect wondering exactly what you will say next. And what do you say? You explain that you can provide the company with a lower total cost solution, thus improving the profitability of the organization. Do you think that your prospect is interested? Of course he is! You then go for the appointment. This response works well for upper management because it directly addresses their primary mandate: to increase the profitability of their organization. A letter to support your script and response has been included in Figure 9-7.

We Have an Existing Relationship

This objection of prospects telling you that they have an existing relationship with one or more of your competitors should also arise quite frequently and is really no different than the response of prospects handling the need for your product or service internally. Referring to Figure 9-2, the prospect is simply telling you that he has filled the core need for your product or service. Your goal, in this instance, should be to identify a niche, or unfilled need. The response outlined in Figure 9-8 would be appropriate when you encounter this objection. A supporting letter is provided in Figure 9-9.

Should prospects question your ability to supplement their existing relationships, your unique selling points will provide

Figure 9-7. Sample follow-up letter for responding to the "we handle the need for your product [service] internally" objection—upper management approach.

July 5, 19XX

Mr. Michael Martinez
Chief Financial Officer
Farefront Corporation
222 Market Street
San Francisco, CA 91111

Dear Mr. Martinez:

It was a pleasure to speak with you today. As we had discussed, we have worked with a number of large organizations like yours and have found that outsourcing can be a cost-effective alternative. For example, recently our company was able to save another large organization more than $100,000 through outsourcing. We have found that many organizations like yours view outsourcing as a cost-effective alternative and I thought it might be of value to you. I would like to stop by at your convenience to introduce myself and share with you details of our outsourcing alternative.

I have enclosed some corporate literature for your review and will be contacting you shortly to reassess your interest in our company. In the interim, should you require additional information or have any questions, please do not hesitate to contact me.

Yours very truly,

Paul Robertson
Senior Account Executive

Figure 9-8. Sample script for responding to the "we have an existing relationship" objection.

Great! That was exactly my reason for the call. We have worked with a number of large organizations like yours and have found that we can be an effective supplement to the services already provided by your primary supplier. I'm going to be in your area on November 2 and would like to stop by to show you how. Are you available at 3:00?

---

you with plenty of ammunition, as they did when we encountered this objection based on the internal resources of the prospects. If you are lucky enough to know which of your competitors the target company is working with, you may want to consider tailoring your response to focus on those unique selling points that highlight your strengths vis-à-vis the competition. Further, a prospect already using a competitor is, in many ways, better than a prospect who does not use your type of product or service at all. A company already using your type of product or service believes in the value of your industry. Your competitor has already done much of your work for you. All you have to do is identify your niche, earn the right to advance, and continue to move further through the sales cycle.

I'm Not the Person Responsible for This

Often, in trying to locate the person responsible for purchasing your product or service, you come upon people who aren't the right contact. This will come into play most often when you work a list without contact names. Using a list without contact names is perhaps the most dreaded task in all of selling. You not only have to cold call to get the appointment but you also have to search for the name of the definitive decision maker. Most salespeople find this a difficult task to overcome. However, if handled properly, it can be the most direct and effective route to take when prospecting. Here's why.

First, you have no preconceptions about the prospect. I'm certain that all of us have avoided contacts either because they

Figure 9-9. Sample follow-up letter for responding to the "we have an existing relationship" objection.

October 15, 19XX

Mr. William Goodman
Executive Vice President
Industrial Rivet and Washer Company
1010 Gills Lane
Nanuet, NY 10509

Dear Mr. Goodman:

It was a pleasure to speak with you today. As we discussed, we have worked with a number of large organizations like yours and have found that we can be an effective supplement to the services you already receive through your primary provider.

For example, recently our company opened a new research and development testing facility to support our first-to-market commitment. Not only does this facility support our internal research and development efforts, but we have also allowed our customers the opportunity to use our facility to test potential applications prior to full-scale production. We have found that many organizations like yours view this as a major benefit of doing business with us and I thought it might be of value to you. I would like to stop by at your convenience to introduce myself and share with you other areas in which we might be able to supplement your primary provider.

I have enclosed some corporate literature for your review and will be contacting you shortly to reassess your interest in our company. In the interim, should you require additional information or have any questions, please do not hesitate to contact me.

Yours very truly,

Leslie Maserjian
Senior Account Manager

were difficult to work with or because we had bad experiences with them in the past. What I found when I finally did call back was often these old contacts were no longer in the same position and I could start working with new contacts. Had I taken the time to verify my assumptions, I could have reduced the length of my sales cycle tremendously.

Second, I'm also sure that all of us have called on people who were not the decision maker for the product or service we were selling. However, because you thought they were the decision maker, you kept trying, which can be a big time waster. Had you taken a few moments to verify your assumptions, you might have been quite a bit more effective.

When you have a list with no names, your expectations of success are not as high because you are starting from a position of limited information and strength. Just like the underdog in sports, you have very little to lose so you go out and give it your best. Often, the result is a performance far above your standard abilities.

The first step in using a list without names is to take the list and rank the prospects according to the demographic factor that best defines your target market as outlined in Chapter 5. By ranking your prospects according to the demographic factor that best defines your target market, you are sure to work with the highest-impact prospects first. This will, of course, lead to you maximizing your return on investment.

Then, call the general number for the prospect company in question. Try to reach a receptionist, operator, or secretary and solicit their support in finding the person responsible for what you sell. My wife, Susan, sells eyewear for Silhouette Optical. If she were trying to find the person responsible for purchasing eyeglass frames at an optician in her target market, the conversation depicted in Figure 9-10 would be appropriate.

This approach is successful because you have taken the time to identify yourself. People are very reluctant to give information to strangers. Because you have taken the time to identify yourself, you have overcome the first hurdle in your path. Also, you are soliciting their help, not making a demand. When you solicit someone's support, my experience has been that they respond in a positive manner. When you place a demand on someone,

Figure 9-10. Sample script for locating the proper decision maker in a company.

Hello, this is Susan Goldner of Silhouette Optical. I was wondering if you could help me please? (A long pause.) I was looking for the person responsible for purchasing eyeglass frames within your company. Do you know who that might be? (Person responds.) Great! Before you transfer me, I was hoping you could provide me with a name and extension in case we get disconnected. Thank you for your help.

my experience has been just the opposite. Saying "I was wondering if you could help me please?" is the most powerful element in the script and greatly increases your probability of success at this point. The long pause requires a response. When you think about it, what are the chances of someone refusing to help you? When possible, it is also important to get the name and phone number or extension of the person to whom you are being transferred.

Once you get transferred, you need to determine whether you have reached the proper person. The script outlined in Figure 9-11 will give you this information. If you have reached the appropriate person, you can move directly into your basic script. If not, apologize for the misunderstanding and ask to be directed to the correct person. I find that you are typically transferred to the correct party about 80 to 90 percent of the time. This estimate is no exaggeration and is why I said that this is quite possibly the best way to prospect. It is the shortest distance between you and the definitive decision maker at the target company.

Figure 9-11. Sample script for verifying that you have reached the proper decision maker in a company.

Yes, Ms. Smith. This is Susan Goldner of Silhouette Optical. How are you today? Great! The reason I am calling is that they transferred me to you and said that you were the person responsible for frame purchases at your company.

Occasionally, you will come across an uncooperative receptionist. When this happens you can usually manipulate the general phone number to direct dial an employee other than the receptionist. For example, if the general corporate number is 867-5000, simply replace the final zero with a number, selected at random, between one and nine. In other words, instead of dialing 867-5000, dial 867-5005 and reach an unknown employee. By selecting a number at random, you almost certainly won't reach the person you are looking for. Continue until you get a live person on the line. You know in advance that you are going to reach the wrong person, so be prepared for the conversation.

A second technique to get past an uncooperative receptionist is to make up a name, say Mary Jones or Bill Smith. The conversation with the receptionist should proceed along the lines outlined in Figure 9-12. If the receptionist is not aware of who handles the purchase decision for your product or service, simply ask to be transferred to the human resource or personnel department. Once again, proceed as detailed above when addressing a wrong contact.

We Do Not Have the Budget for Your Product or Service

My first thought when encountering this objection is to reflect on the Selling Life-Cycle Paradigm. Remember, selling is a pro-

Figure 9-12. Second script for locating the proper decision maker in a company.

Receptionist: Gordon Industries. How may I help you?
You: Bill Smith please.
Receptionist: I'm sorry, we don't have a Bill Smith working at this company.
You: Maybe you can help me. I used to work with Bill in the area of office supplies. I was wondering if you could direct me to the person responsible for that function within your company now.
Receptionist: Sure. Let me transfer you to Harry Stevens.
You: Thank you. You've been most helpful.

cess and not an event. Given this long-term view of the sales cycle, you cannot expect an immediate return from every client and prospect. However, since you are working within *your* target market, every call is a quality call and every prospect is a quality prospect. You cannot hurt yourself by developing an account within your target market, no matter how long the account cycle might be for the prospect. Given that a prospect did not properly budget for your product or service, now might be the best time to start building a relationship. If this is the case, you may want to consider the approach outlined in Figure 9-13. Your supporting letter is provided in Figure 9-14. Personal relationships are the strongest relationships and this strategy will pay handsome long-run dividends for you.

A second approach that you may want to consider is to reflect on the fact that your objective, as a professional salesperson, is to improve your customers' profitability, not detract from it. You must ask yourself, "How can my product or service benefit the prospect?" You should be able to provide some concrete answers to this question. For example, will your product or service improve productivity? Will it decrease expenses? Will it increase the performance of the sales force? There are a number of ways in which you can be of great value to prospects. Once you have identified the benefits you bring to the table, you might respond as outlined in Figure 9-15.

We are using a very popular sales technique. It is know as the "Feel, Felt, Found" or the "Repeat, Reassure, Resume" technique. The foundation of this technique is that one of the most powerful motivating forces supporting one's decision to buy or not to buy is the fear of failure. Your response tells the prospect that there are others out there that are in exactly the same posi-

Figure 9-13. Sample script for responding to the "we have no budget" objection.

Ms. Chang, I understand that you may have current budget constraints. However, my goal is not necessarily to sell you something today, but rather, to build a lasting relationship. I'm going to be in your area on January 6 and would like to stop by. Are you available at 3:00?

Figure 9-14. Sample follow-up letter for responding to the "we have no budget" objection.

January 2, 19XX

Ms. Jacqueline Chang
Director of Purchasing
JEG International
10 South Street
Portland, OR 98811

Dear Ms. Chang:

It was a pleasure to speak with you today. While I understand that the time might not be right to make a purchase of this nature now, I did want to take the time to introduce you to our organization. Many organizations like yours have grown to be some of our best customers and I would like to start building our relationship now.

I have enclosed some corporate literature for your review and will be contacting you in the future to reassess your interest in our company. In the interim, should you require additional information or have any questions, please do not hesitate to contact me.

Yours very truly,

Elissa Goldsmith
Senior Account Executive

Figure 9-15. Second sample script for responding to the "we have no budget" objection.

Ms. Chang, we have worked with a number of organizations in your exact position. In fact, they felt exactly as you did prior to spending a few moments with us. I'm going to be in your area on June 25 and would like to stop by. Are you available at 3:00?

tion; that they reacted similarly, and once they understand the nature of the offer, they will likely feel different as well. This powerful technique can be used to turn around many objections, whether over the telephone or in face-to-face sales meetings. The key to using this technique again lies in preparation. If the prospect asks just how you might be of value, be prepared to respond.

Your Price Is Too High

The all-important objection to price eventually surfaces in every sales situation. First of all, if your price is truly too high, nobody would buy your product or service and your company would go out of business. In addition, price is a relative issue, not an absolute one. Your job, therefore, is to show that your product or service warrants the price you are charging. When questioned about the price of a product or service, I try to agree with the prospect. I allow that we are not the lowest-priced organization on the market. We are well aware of that. On the other hand, we are not the highest-priced either. In all likelihood, there will always be someone in the market with a higher price than yours and there will also always be someone in the market with a lower price than yours.

Your job is to establish value, not to discuss price. In fact, your customers should be in search of the lowest total cost solution, not the lowest price. The difference can be quite significant. Consider the following tale as an example.

Assume that you had the opportunity to purchase one of two certificates of deposit. The first certificate costs you $100 and yields 5 percent. The second certificate costs you $500 and yields 15 percent. Which certificate would you prefer, the cheaper one or the more expensive one? The answer is always the same. You would rather purchase the $500 certificate because the more expensive certificate is worth the price. Your job is now to show that your product or service is worth the premium you are charging. Taking this one step further, as I would expect any sophisticated buyer to do, your job is also to establish that the initial purchase price is only one element in the total cost of ownership of a product or service. For example, assume that you went to a store to buy a suit and there were two suits that caught your eye, one for $200 and a second for $300. You really only have $200 to spend. Which suit might be the more appropriate purchase?

At first glance, you might conclude the $200 suit would be better for you. However, if you examine the facts a little closer, you might reach a different conclusion. A typical suit may last you approximately two years under normal conditions. If the more expensive suit is of higher quality, it may require that you bring the suit to the cleaner once a month. The less expensive suit may need to be cleaned and pressed after each wearing or once a week. If it costs $10 to clean a suit, you can see that the total cost of ownership for the less expensive suit amounts to $1,240: the original cost of the suit ($200) plus the weekly cleaning bill over a two-year period ($1,040). The total cost of ownership of the more expensive suit amounts to only $540: the original cost of the suit ($300) plus the monthly cleaning bill over a two-year period ($240). As you can see, a close study of the facts may lead you to a different conclusion.

One of my clients makes extruders, which are extremely expensive pieces of equipment that melt little plastic pellets so the plastic can be used to coat a variety of products including diapers and potato chip bags. An extruder costs anywhere from $500,000 to $5 million. The company I was working with was the oldest and most established company in the industry. However, it was suffering from severe foreign price competition. Often the foreign competition would price a "comparable" product at 40 percent less than my client's product. My client had to establish very quickly that the price of the product was only one small element of the total cost of ownership. Here's how he did it.

First, my client was the oldest and most established company in the industry. The company had been in business more than a century and produced machines that it had sold more than twenty-five years ago that were still in operation. The company's foreign competition was comprised of smaller, thinly capitalized companies whose machinery was lasting an average of only five to ten years.

Suppose, for example, that my client had an opportunity to sell a particular extruder for $1 million. The foreign competition might price a "similar" product at, say, $600,000. Quite a difference! However, my client's machines were lasting at least twice as long as the competition's. Thus, over a twenty-year period, the competition's machine could cost as little as $1.2 million if it only had to be replaced once (the best-case scenario) and as high as $3 million if it had to be replaced six times (the worst-case scenario). Which machine is truly the lower cost alternative?

To further support its argument, my client was more likely to be able to honor its warranty because the foreign competition was often thinly capitalized. In fact, many of the foreign competitors went out of business after only a few years. As one would go out of business, a new foreign company would pop up. Prospects could see that in making an acquisition priced from $500,000 to $5 million, they would want the company they bought the machine from to be in business long enough to honor warranties and service the equipment. If not, they would be faced with having to replace the entire machine, a costly alternative.

The third point that my client emphasized was the cost of servicing broken equipment. Downtime for an extruder costs a company approximately $20,000 per hour. My client was able to provide next-day parts and service whereas a foreign competitor might take a week or more. One breakdown a year would more than justify the price differential in the initial purchase.

Given the preceding examples, you might consider the response to the price objection outlined in Figure 9-16. Figure 9-17 provides your written response to the price objection. In order to close this call, you would then quickly review your company's

**Figure 9-16. Sample script for responding to the
"price" objection.**

Mr. Jackson, price is a concern to all of us. However, we work with a
number of large organizations just like yours who believe that they receive
an appropriate return on their investment with our company.

---

unique selling points as they relate to providing the target company with the lowest total-cost solution. A salesperson for the
company selling extruder equipment needs to mention several
elements that enter into the total cost of ownership of an extruder: the durability of the equipment, the stability of the organization, the company's ability to honor warranties, and the
ability to provide timely service. The salesperson's close might
be, "I'm going to be in your area on June 23 and would like to
stop by to discuss how these factors might enter into your decision. Are you available at 3:00?"

Your response should tell the prospect two things: first, that
other organizations like his have felt that your services were
worth the price you charge (remember Feel, Felt, Found); second, why you're worth what you charge (your unique selling
points). Respond to concerns without getting into a lengthy debate over the phone. Commandment 3 advises you to keep your
calls brief. Your goal is to respond as quickly and as efficiently
as possible to each objection, then get the appointment. You will
have ample opportunity in the face-to-face selling environment
to establish value.

We Have Used Your Company in the Past and Were Dissatisfied

Hopefully, this objection is not encountered too frequently. If
your company is doing a good job of servicing its customers, it
will survive and prosper. If not, the market will tell you this and
your company will ultimately go out of business. The fact is that
most companies that survive in today's increasingly competitive
market do a good job of servicing their customer base most of

Figure 9-17. Sample follow-up letter for responding to the "price" objection.

June 12, 19XX

Mr. Steven Jackson
Purchasing Manager
Credit Card Incorporated
10 Wall Street
New York, NY 10001

Dear Mr. Jackson:

It was a pleasure to speak with you today. While I understand that you may have some concerns about our product pricing, I would still like to stop by and introduce you to our organization. Many companies shared your same concerns prior to fully understanding our product offering. In fact, many of these companies have grown to be some of our best customers and I would like to start building our relationship now.

I have enclosed some corporate literature for your review and will be contacting you in the future to reassess your interest in our company. In the interim, should you require additional information or have any questions, please do not hesitate to contact me.

Yours very truly,

Jack Arthur
Senior Account Executive

the time. However, mistakes do happen and problems do arise. When they do, you must be prepared to respond. In fact, I would venture to say that most customers judge your company and you by the way you respond to adversity more than by the way you respond when things are going along smoothly.

When working with a dissatisfied customer, I like to rely on advice put forth by Dale Carnegie more than half a century ago. His principle for handling complaints is to "Let the other person do a great deal of the talking." This instruction is so appealing because it is consistent with the ideal of consultative selling, to let the customer or prospect do most of the talking. Our role is to listen, take good notes, analyze the facts, and then make great recommendations.

Dale Carnegie thought that most people try to win others to their point of view by doing all of the talking. His strategy was to ask the other person a question—the key element in the consultative sales process—and let the aggrieved party explain what was bothering her. In short, his advice is to let the other person do most of the talking because she knows more about her problems (or needs) than you do.

A dissatisfied customer essentially has an unfilled need. So do all prospects! Your job is to immediately address the prospect and the problem (or need) head-on. An effective response to this concern is outlined in Figure 9-18. The prospect will tell you about the problem. Your job is to listen attentively and take notes. Not only will you be able to satisfy the needs of this customer, but you will also learn how to satisfy the needs of other customers who feel the same way about your company. The bottom line is that you must rectify the problem *at any cost*. The reason is known as the "Law of 250," which states that each person knows 250 other people. Do something right for a person

Figure 9-18. Sample script for responding to a dissatisfied customer or prospect.

Ms. Jones, I'm glad I was able to get in touch with you. Please take a few moments to tell me about the source of your dissatisfaction.

and she is likely to tell other people. Do something wrong to a person and she is sure to tell everyone she knows. The power of word of mouth is incredible. Think about the last new restaurant you went to. You probably went on the recommendation of a friend. After hearing about the problem, you might respond as outlined in Figure 9-19. Figure 9-20 contains your written response. A dissatisfied customer represents a wonderful selling opportunity.

Can You Turn Around Every Objection?

These examples show that it pays to be prepared for objections. They are going to come and should not overwhelm you. You can develop simple, well-thought-out responses to all objections. Please note that these responses have substance as well as thought. When you actually analyze your response, you are helping make your customer or prospect better off. If you can help your customer or prospect become better off, you should be an evangelist for your product or service. You have nothing to be ashamed of and should aggressively pursue your business opportunities.

At this point, you might also be wondering if all objections can be overcome. The answer to this question is obviously "NO." By preparing for objections we are assisting you in developing thoughtful responses that will enhance your probability of success during the prospecting process. Remember, if the prospect doesn't want to meet with you, there is really nothing that you can do to change that. However, finding out this information (as soon as possible) is a positive event. Now you can

Figure 9-19. Addition to sample script for responding to a dissatisfied customer or prospect.

Ms. Jones, I understand your problem and would like to make amends. In fact, if I were you, I'd feel exactly the same way as you do. I'm going to be in your neighborhood on September 19. Are you available at three?

Figure 9-20. Sample follow-up letter for responding to a dissatisfied customer or prospect.

September 10, 19XX

Ms. Jori Jones
Sales Manager
ACME Tire and Tube
15 North Salem Avenue
Boston, MA 06000

Dear Ms. Jones:

I am glad that I was able to speak with you today. I am very concerned about your perceptions and would like to stop by your office to better understand them. Zebra Systems is very proud of its products and will do whatever is necessary to support them.

I have enclosed some corporate literature for your review and will be contacting you in the future to reassess your interest in our company. In the interim, should you require additional information or have any questions, please do not hesitate to contact me.

Yours very truly,

Taryn Keith
Senior Account Executive

properly position this prospect in your sales pipeline and focus the lion's share of your efforts on finding those prospects in your target market who are ready, willing, and able to buy now.

I will always try twice on the same call to turn around the prospect's objections and get the appointment. After that, the conversation becomes strained and unnatural. Remember, you may want to call this prospect back again at some later date. In fact, you surely will. So don't burn any bridges. Once I have made two attempts on the same call to turn around the objection and have been unsuccessful, I simply tell the prospect that I will keep him on our mailing list and follow up at a later date to see if things have changed. This tack does two things for you. First, it confirms the fact that the prospect is interested in your product or service. If the company has absolutely no interest, it will ask to be removed from the mailing list. Second, you open the door for your follow-up call, where you have some really great opportunities.

At this point, you made two bona fide attempts at getting the appointment and were unsuccessful. The question then becomes, What do you say on your follow-up calls? My experience has been that if you say or do the same thing, you will likely experience the same result—another rejection. I like to believe that the prospect did not give you an appointment on the first call because you did not uncover a need. Therefore, our approach to follow-up calls should be very similar to that outlined in the preceding chapter. The prospect needs to be placed in the Business Development Cycle. This way, each time you call the prospect, you will be presenting him with a new reason to meet with you. Your prospecting strategy, as it relates to overcoming objections, is presented in Figure 9-21. My first follow-up call would then relate to my first unique selling point. Using our manufacturer of high-technology office equipment, Office Tech, the conversation might proceed as indicated in Figure 9-22. In reviewing Figure 9-22, you should notice that this is the same script we presented in the prior chapter relating to Office Tech's first unique selling point. The only difference is the introduction to the script, which reminds the prospect of the fact that you have already spoken and that you are following up on the prior conversation you had.

Figure 9-21. Prospecting strategy for overcoming objections.

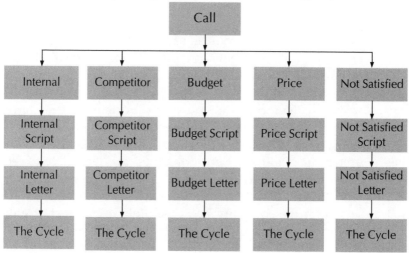

Figure 9-22. Sample script for your second attempt at penetrating a target account.

Mr. Jones, this is Susan Simms of Office Tech. How are you today? Great! The reason I am calling is that we had spoken back on September 15 and you had asked me to follow up with you at this time. As you may know, we were recently FIRST TO MARKET with a new piece of high-technology office equipment that will revolutionize the way companies do business. We have successfully installed this machine at a number of organizations like yours and I would like to come by and demonstrate it to you. I'm going to be in your area on October 30 and would like to stop by. Are you available at 3:00?

This approach will yield excellent results. Typically, the prospect will not remember your initial conversation. However, by following up, the prospect will assume that he asked you to do so. Since this is your second call, he also realizes that he has put you off once already and it probably wouldn't be polite to do so again. Further, he assumes that since he asked you to call back, he must have a need for your product or service. You usually get the appointment. However, if you don't get the appointment, don't get emotional. Just schedule the prospect for an additional follow-up call and move on to your next unique selling point.

The previous chapter outlined the first element of our business development strategy: what to do when you reach the prospect and get the appointment. This chapter outlined a strategy for overcoming the objections you might encounter in the business development and prospecting process. The next chapter is going to complete our strategy by outlining an approach for when you do not reach the prospect you intended to call—in other words, what to do when you encounter voice mail or a secretary.

10

Working With Voice Mail, Administrative Assistants, and Secretaries

This chapter brings our prospecting and business development strategy full circle. Chapters 7 and 8 discussed what to do when you reach the person you were intending to reach and get the appointment. Chapter 9 talked about overcoming objections—what to do when you reach the person you were intending to reach and do not get the appointment. This chapter outlines a strategy that will allow you to work with both voice mail and secretaries or administrative assistants. You will learn techniques you can use when you do not reach the person you were intending to reach when you made the call.

Working With Voice Mail

Voice mail is a fairly recent introduction to the world of professional selling and can be a great source of frustration. Unfortunately, most salespeople have not developed a thoughtful strategy for how to respond to voice mail. It is often viewed as the ultimate gatekeeper. An alternative is to view voice mail as the ultimate advertising vehicle.

Voice mail gives you an unfettered opportunity to deliver a message. By unfettered, I mean that you can present your position without interruption or objection. In fact, this may be the only time in your life that you will have the opportunity to speak and not have someone present an alternative position. Because you have an opportunity to speak without interruption, you need to have an approach or strategy prepared. In fact, you ought to have an advertising campaign. Working with voice mail then becomes a matter of what to place in your advertising campaign. Once again, your five unique selling points will provide you with plenty of ammunition. These unique selling points can be the basis for your company's voice-mail advertising campaign. Each time you call the prospect, leave one of the following messages, in sequence:

First call:	Introductory message
Second call:	Message relating to unique selling point number 1
Third call:	Message relating to unique selling point number 2
Fourth call:	Message relating to unique selling point number 3
Fifth call:	Message relating to unique selling point number 4
Sixth call:	Message relating to unique selling point number 5

The plan, in working with voice mail, is to immediately place your prospect in the Business Development Cycle as shown in Figure 10-1. Figure 10-1 is identical to the Business Development Cycle that we presented in Chapter 8. Here, we must slightly modify the contents of both our unique selling point letters and scripts and also introduce a script for the introductory portion of the Business Development Cycle. The modifications to your unique selling points scripts and letters are minimal so I have only recrafted one letter and one script to serve as an example. These are presented in Figures 10-2 and 10-3, respectively. The introductory script and letter would be based on your basic script and is presented in Figures 10-4 and 10-5, respectively. Please note that the introductory voice mail script is used on your first call to a prospect, when you reach voice mail.

It is important to reemphasize that this strategy gives you either six months, eighteen months, or thirty-six months worth

Figure 10-1. Business development strategy reprise.

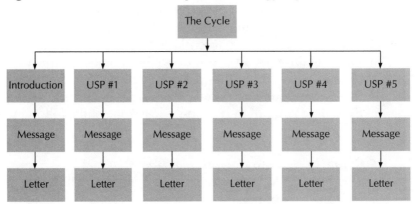

Figure 10-2. Sample script for first unique selling point voice mail message.

This is Susan Simms of Office Tech. The reason I'm calling is because we were recently FIRST TO MARKET with a new piece of high-technology office equipment that will revolutionize the way companies do business. We have successfully installed this machine at a number of organizations like yours and I would like to come by and demonstrate it to you. Please give me a call at 212-555-1212 so that we may set up a mutually convenient meeting time. Thank you very much and have a great day.

---

of voice mail messages if you follow the callback periods recommended in Chapter 5. Further, the Business Development Cycle is reusable in that when you reach the end of your first series of messages, simply go back to the beginning and slightly alter the focus of each of your original messages. After all, if your company was first to market with a product six months ago, you may have a new first-to-market product introduction the next time you need to use this unique selling point message.

After you have left your carefully prepared advertising message on the voice mail of the decision maker, you may want to consider immediately calling back. This time, however, you are not calling to leave a message, but rather to speak to the decision

Figure 10-3. Sample follow-up letter for first unique selling point voice mail message.

February 20, 19XX

Mr. Robert Jones
Director of Administration
NYT International
15 South Salem Avenue
Lower Newton Falls, MA 06000

Dear Mr. Jones:

Recently, I gave you a call to introduce a new piece of high-technology office equipment that will revolutionize the way companies do business. The release of this new product demonstrates our continued commitment to be First to Market with new high-technology office equipment.

Given the size of your organization and your commitment to provide state-of-the-art products to your customers, I thought this new equipment might be of value to you. We are seeing a strong growth trend in this area among our largest corporate accounts.

I have enclosed some product literature for your review and will be contacting you shortly to discuss your interest in this program. In the interim, should you require additional information or have any questions, please do not hesitate to contact me.

Yours very truly,

Susan Simms
Account Manager

Figure 10-4. Sample script for introductory voice mail message.

This is Susan Simms of Office Tech. The reason I'm calling is because I sent you some information about our organization in the mail. We provide high-technology office equipment to large corporations like yours and I would like to stop by and introduce myself. Please give me a call at 212-555-1212 so that we may arrange for a mutually convenient time. Thank you very much and have a great day.

---

maker's secretary. Here, follow the strategy outlined in the following section. At a minimum, you want to make certain that you are addressing the proper decision maker.

When working with voice mail, there are several additional key ingredients, gleaned from the Ten Commandments of Prospecting, that will improve your chances of success: be persistent, vary your call times, try nontraditional hours, and always earn the right to advance. Your voice mail advertising campaign should be supplemented by focused letters, again bringing out your unique selling points, corporate mailings, and handwritten notes highlighting articles of interest to the prospect.

Working With Administrative Assistants or Secretaries

Administrative assistants or secretaries also seem to be a great source of frustration for many sales professionals. The key to working with administrative assistants is to understand their role in the sales process. When you reach an administrative assistant instead of a decision maker, you must understand that what has changed is the level of the sale. You must still make a sale, however. Please consider Figure 10-6. For purposes of this discussion, I am defining product and service sales as tangible transactions because they result in a physical transaction in which funds are exchanged in return for either goods or services.

Figure 10-5. Sample follow-up letter for introductory voice mail message.

February 20, 19XX

Mr. Robert Jones
Director of Administration
NYT International
15 South Salem Avenue
Lower Newton Falls, MA 06000

Dear Mr. Jones:

    Recently, I gave you a call to introduce you to our company. We provide high-technology office equipment to large corporations like yours and I would like to stop by and introduce myself. I have enclosed some corporate literature for your review and will be contacting you shortly to discuss your interest in our company. In the interim, should you require additional information or have any questions, please do not hesitate to contact me.

Yours very truly,

Susan Simms
Account Manager

Figure 10-6. Different levels of a sale for working with administrative assistants.

Sale Level	Sale Type
Product or Service	Tangible
Appointment	Conceptual
Pre-Appointment	Conceptual

Administrative assistants simply add a third level to the sales process. When you reach an administrative assistant instead of a decision maker, the nature of the conceptual sale changes. Instead of making the goal of your prospecting call to get an appointment with the decision maker, you must change the goal of the call to having the secretary allow you to talk to the decision maker.

The best strategy for reaching the decision maker is to work with the administrative assistant, not around him. The first thing I always do is ask the assistant his name. This can be tremendously flattering, especially when you consider how secretaries are treated by many organizations and salespeople. Once I have learned the name of the secretary, I immediately record it in my computerized contact management system. Thus, when I call back, I can immediately address the secretary by name.

I do not recommend investing time in setting up face-to-face meetings with secretaries since you can do some very effective work over the telephone. I have found most secretaries to be extremely knowledgeable in their boss's business affairs. In my business—the training business—the secretary would have an understanding of computer training.

When you reach a secretary, the conversation might go as depicted in Figure 10-7. Very often the secretary can provide you with a wealth of valuable information at this point. Always try to confirm the fact that the secretary's boss is the true decision maker for your product or service. I can't tell you how much time I've spent in my career chasing after people who were not the decision maker for my product. You don't get as many return calls as you would like when you are calling a person who

Figure 10-7. Initial script for working with secretaries.

Secretary: Mr. Venturini's office. How may I help you?
You: Mr. Venturini please.
Secretary: I'm sorry, Mr. Venturini is in a meeting right now. May I take a message and have him get back to you?
You: Yes, this is Elissa Gabriel of Future Vision. Would you mind telling me your name please?
Secretary: This is Adam.
You: Yes, Adam, how are you today?
Secretary: Fine.
You: I'm sorry, I didn't hear your last name.
Secretary: Smith.
You: Adam, the reason I'm calling is to follow up on the information I sent to Mr. Venturini. Our company provides duplicating services to large organizations like yours and I just wanted to see how your company handles its needs for those types of services. Is Mr. Venturini the decision maker in this area?
Secretary: Yes he is.
You: Great! Before I speak with Mr. Venturini, can you tell me a little bit about how you handle your needs in this area?

has no interest in what you are selling! Secretaries can also tell you about their companies' current needs, future direction, which of your competitors they are using, and many other helpful pieces of information. After hearing the secretary's response and recording as much detail as possible in your contact management system, several approaches are possible.

First, secretaries are often empowered to make decisions and appointments on behalf of their bosses. If this is the case, the response in Figure 10-8 may be appropriate. Remember the movie *Wall Street*. It was the secretary who got Charlie Sheen his first appointment with Michael Douglas.

Unfortunately, not all secretaries are willing to make an appointment for their boss. If this is the case, you might try the approach outlined in Figure 10-9. We are learning both when are the best times to reach Mr. Venturini and trying to set up a telephone appointment. This will allow us to move to the second step on the sales ladder. In closing, you might also want to

Figure 10-8. First supplemental script for working with secretaries.

Adam, I'm going to be in your area next Tuesday at 3:00. The reason I was calling is to set up an appointment with Mr. Venturini. Can you look at his schedule and see if he is available at that time? He is. Great! I'm going to put this appointment in my calendar. Would you please confirm this appointment with Mr. Venturini and call me back to confirm. I'll also call the day before to confirm as well. Thank you very much. I look forward to meeting you next Tuesday.

Figure 10-9. Second supplemental script for working with secretaries.

Adam, I'd like to speak with Mr. Venturini at a time that is more convenient for him. Is there a best time to reach Mr. Venturini? Would it be appropriate to set up a telephone appointment now?

strongly consider leaving times that are best to call you back, to minimize the amount of telephone tag that you play.

If neither of the foregoing approaches work, you can consider the fallback position presented in Figure 10-10. Remember, if the secretary will not allow you to meet with or talk to the boss, your next best alternative is to change the level of the sale and see if you can first sell the secretary on letting you through to the boss. The key to this approach is not to think of secretaries

Figure 10-10. Third supplemental script for working with secretaries.

Adam, I have already sent our corporate literature to Mr. Venturini. What I'd like to do is send you a copy and then call you back to discuss it after you have had a chance to review this information. This will allow you to determine if it would be appropriate for me to meet Mr. Venturini.

as just corporate gatekeepers. It has very condescending implications and can serve to increase the barriers between you and the true decision maker. Secretaries are there to help. They are there to help the person for whom they work and they can be very helpful to you as well. Further, you never know where that secretary will wind up. Someday, he could be a decision maker at the company he presently works for or at another large organization. By winning the confidence of the secretary, you can work together to solve a common problem: how to get the decision maker and you together for a phone conversation or meeting.

If you are not successful, you can always refer back to the Ten Commandments of Prospecting. First, remember to call at off-peak hours. Decision makers often work at times when secretaries do not: 8:00 to 9:00 A.M., noon to 1:00 P.M., and 5:00 to 6:00 P.M. are great cold calling hours. Also, don't forget the "golden minute": 11:59 A.M. This is the single best minute to cold call during the entire day. Second, remember to vary your call times. People are creatures of habit and are often doing the same thing at the same time, each and every day. By varying your call times, you will catch both the decision maker and the secretary at different moments in their daily and weekly routines. Third, don't get emotional or discouraged. We are only talking about a dial of the phone. It's up to you to be persistent, to keep on trying. If you are persistent, you will eventually get through.

Finally, your prospects are not sitting around waiting for your call. You must *earn the right* to work with your prospects. If you are having no luck on the telephone, consider sending a well-worded letter with some corporate literature. Overnight mail often has a greater impact than does regular mail. Fax mail also works quite well. Keep your eye open for articles on your prospect's company. Clip the articles and send them to the prospect with a brief handwritten cover letter. Over time, these will surely earn you the right to advance.

We have spent the last several chapters outlining a business development strategy that will increase your probability of success in the sales cycle. There are two more ideas, however, that we can use to make us more successful: engage in practices that will make your prospects come to you, the subject of the next chapter, and learn from experience, the subject of the final chapter. So, let's move on!

11

Public Relations: How to Make Your Prospects Come to You

Thus far, we have worked exclusively with ideas that proactively help you penetrate a particular prospect within your target market. These ideas are crucial to your success and will certainly contribute to the probability of a positive outcome in the sales process. However, public relations tools, such as press releases, newsletters, public speaking engagements, and networking, can also be very powerful allies in your quest for selling success. A well-planned public relations campaign can position you as an industry expert and create excitement about what you do, building a mystique about you and your product. Opportunity will begin to chase you for a change.

Press Releases

When most people think of public relations, they think of both the cost and expense of hiring a public relations firm. Believe it or not, you can be your own public relations firm. All you need to begin is a list of names to send press releases to and a press release. Build your list of names with the definitive decision makers at your high-priority accounts. If you remember, a high-priority account in your target market would be most likely to buy large quantities of your product or service. You can also add local business and trade publications in your market, as well as producers of local television and radio shows.

Send releases to the editor-in-chief of trade and business publications. The address of the editorial offices and the editor's name are always listed on one of the first pages. Releases should be sent to producers of shows that cover your industry on local television and radio stations. The producers' names are usually listed in the credits at the end of each show. Develop this list over time, and work to keep it current. The media industry is prone to change, and you want your list to be as accurate as possible. The information is all free and readily available.

Once you have compiled your list of accounts and media outlets, send one press release per month. More frequent mailings would dilute the effect of your release. Less frequent mailings precipitate the old adage, "Out of sight, out of mind." Your release topics should be based on your unique selling points and should be coordinated with your prospecting and voice mail activities.

To prepare press releases it is important to include these five key elements:

1. Your name, company, and address
2. The release date
3. The headline
4. The dateline (city of origin)
5. The body of the release

For an excellent in-depth discussion of how to write a press release, refer to Paul Karasik's *How to Make It Big in the Seminar Business.* Keep your releases brief—one page if possible—and interesting. A sample press release announcing a new product introduction is included in Figure 11-1.

Newsletters

Another publicity tool that will work well is to create your own newsletter. If your company does this for you, that's great. However, if it doesn't prepare a newsletter, consider preparing one yourself and distributing the newsletter to the names on the list that you personally manage. Depending on the size of your

Figure 11-1. Sample press release relating to one of your unique selling points.

NEWS RELEASE

ABC Publishing Company
555 Cherry Hill Road
Port Charles, NY 55555

ABC Publishing Company
Exceeds the 1,000 Title Plateau

For Immediate Release
Thursday 22 September 1994

Contact: Jason Kaufman
914-555-1212

Port Charles—ABC Publishing Company (ABC), an international provider of innovative business titles, announced the release of its one thousandth distinct business title. The ABC titles span not only the conventional business publications such as sales, management, and personal development, but also include a full array of offerings in areas including team-building and excellence programs. "We take great pride in both the depth of our offerings as well as our first-to-market commitment," commented Jason Kaufman, ABC's CEO. "We believe that the combination of these two offerings uniquely positions us to service corporate America."

Founded in 1923, ABC Publishing Company is dedicated to providing the highest-quality business publications in the world. ABC's publications are designed to raise productivity, efficiency, and total quality by increasing employee effectiveness.

mailing list, you may want to consider sending your newsletters to all the names on the list or just a selection of key contacts—or what I like to refer to as definitive decision makers. A newsletter can be a very effective device in positioning you as an industry expert, the value of which cannot be overestimated. I prepare my own quarterly newsletter to promote my sales training and speaking activities and it has been well worth the investment in time.

Remember that providing information to your clients and prospects is one of the ways you can add value to your product or service. The complexity of your product or service and rate at which your product or service changes only serve to make information more and more valuable to your clients over time. Purchasers of goods and services are always looking to improve their position as a result of a purchase decision. Through the newsletter, the salesperson can provide useful information, helping the purchaser maximize the value received from your product.

A newsletter also gives you the opportunity to reach out to many prospects at the same time, and build your reputation as an expert and source of valuable information. However, publishing a newsletter is a time-consuming process, so only prepare to publish on a quarterly basis. Anything more might prove to be too burdensome and anything less would probably dilute the impact of your efforts.

Your newsletter activities should be coordinated with your press releases. During the months that you mail your newsletter, it's best not to send a press release. You do not want to inundate people with too much information at once. If you do, they will tend to get overloaded and probably not digest much, if anything, of the message you delivered. Your newsletter should be no more than four 8½-by-11–inch pages. Print each newsletter on both sides of one sheet of 11-by-17–inch paper, so it can be folded in half and read like a book. This is much neater than stapling pages together. When you choose the paper for the letter, check that it is thick enough to print on both sides without words showing through. Four pages provide enough space for one or two focused articles. The articles should be brief and to the point. They should also provide the reader with one or two nuggets of valuable information. Most people already have a tremendous amount of information they must absorb. I try to give them something extremely valuable that they can absorb in a very brief time frame.

Be sure to keep the information fresh and current. Our company has been sending newsletters for almost ten years now, and over the years I have gotten calls from prospects who had been on our mailing list and consistently received our newsletter. The message was always the same. "Thank you for keeping me on your mailing list. After five years of receiving your newsletter, I finally saw something that might be of value to our company. When can we get together?" That's correct. Definitive decision makers at large organizations called us to do business! The newsletter had finally struck a chord. Once you begin your newsletter, keep sending it. The impact you will create over time will be tremendous. Earlier you read about a man trying to break a rock with a sledge hammer. Ultimately the cumulative effect of the blows broke the rock. A newsletter works in the same manner. Its cumulative effect can be very powerful.

Public Speaking

Following on the theme of reaching out to many prospects at once, public speaking can be a powerful supplement to your sales activities. Speaking in public, like professional selling, is a skill that can be mastered by anyone. Toastmasters International, an organization dedicated to improving your communication and leadership skills, would be an excellent option to anyone interested in improving their speaking skills. The opportunity to speak in front of several hundred decision makers in your industry should be grabbed. Industry conferences are always hungry for speakers. All you have to do is develop a topic of interest and volunteer. Start at the smaller conferences and fine-tune your speech and your skills. Then move on to the major conferences in your industry. Besides increasing your sales opportunities, you'll get to travel and will have fun. The result of your presentations will be inbound requests for additional information. If you reflect on just how hard it is to get an appointment with a pros-

pect, a healthy supplement of inbound requests can be very re-
freshing. Once you obtain a speaking engagement, refrain from
selling your goods and services while on the platform. Focus on
providing valuable information to your audience. The sales will
follow.

Networking

Some might think that networking is an obvious recommendation and not worthy of mention in this book. However, networking can take place at two levels: the obvious and the not so
obvious. The obvious form of networking would be to network
within the industries of your clients and prospects—in other
words, to network within your target market. The benefit of this
type of networking is that it establishes you as a player in the
industry, gives you industry visibility, and allows you to meet
the other players in the industry—your colleagues as well as
your prospects. The negative aspect of this type of networking
is that you always meet the same people and everyone has their
guards up. In other words, they expect you to sell! This precon-
ception can be difficult to overcome.

Networking outside of your target market can be very powerful. This is one additional advantage to membership in Toastmasters, for example. Because the focus of a Toastmasters club
is personal development, and not the sale of your product or
service, the opportunities that tend to develop are more real and
immediate. Country clubs, health clubs, civic organizations, volunteer groups, charities, and other similar organizations can
provide an additional source of prospects and sales opportunities.

Prospecting and business development are hard work. This
chapter was devoted to taking the "chill" out of cold calling by
providing you with some ideas to supplement your direct business development activities. The next chapter focuses on the
final element of our core strategy: leveraging your success with
existing customers to help you find new customers and prospects.

12

How to Leverage Your Success

The first eleven chapters of this book outlined an approach to business development and prospecting that can be employed by anyone, even if it is your first day in sales. Ultimately, however, you will make a sale and this chapter will teach you how to leverage your success to create additional sales opportunities. The key to this approach is to have an existing customer, for whom you have performed well, endorse your product or service. An endorsement is when one person vouches for the credibility of another. We see this all of the time on TV. Companies pay millions of dollars to have stars endorse their products. The reason they do this is that people assume that if the star uses the product, it must be good enough for ordinary folks like you and me.

In professional selling, we can also use an endorsement to enhance the probability of our success in the sales cycle. The value of an endorsement is almost immeasurable. After all, the prospect expects you to say good things about your product or service. In fact, many prospects may take what the salesperson says with a grain of salt or more. However, what prospects don't always expect is a third party, with no vested interest in the sale of your product or service, to give you an endorsement. Further, since the third party receives no financial remuneration as a result of the endorsement, a third-party endorsement in the context of professional selling may have even greater impact than the types of endorsements we are used to seeing on television. No amount of selling on your part can equal the value of even the smallest endorsement from a third party in the eyes of a prospect.

Third-party endorsements can be testimonials from customers inside the target prospect. An endorsement from inside the target prospect organization is perhaps the most powerful endorsement. Here, you are doing work in one area of a company. Assume that it is the pension area. You have just successfully completed a project and you ask the definitive decision maker in the pension area if he is aware of anyone else in the organization that could use your product or service. Since you have just successfully completed a project, the likelihood that the company will give you a reference is quite high if the company is aware of someone with a similar need. If you are referred to another individual within the organization, your cold calling script might look as detailed in Figure 12-1. In reviewing the script, you will of course notice that the script does not vary much from the basic script in Chapter 7. This script, and the endorsement approach, has particular power because each successful company has its own quality standards and any vendor must meet or exceed that quality standard. By virtue of the fact that you have successfully completed a similar project in another area of the company, you have equaled or exceeded the requisite quality standard. Thus, the risk for the new prospect in the sale is greatly reduced and he is more likely to move forward. In other words, your chance of making a sale with an existing cus-

Figure 12-1. First sample script for a "third party endorsement."

Mr. Weineib please. Hello Mr. Weineib. This is Jacqueline Jencine of Maughan Industries. How are you today? Great! The reason that I'm calling is because we just completed a very successful program for your company in the pension area. We were working with Arlene Gersh.

Our company provides a financial information database to large organizations like yours, and Arlene thought that you might have a need for this type of information. How do you handle your needs for this type of information in your area? Great! I'm going to be in your area on May 31 and would like to stop by and introduce myself. Are you available at 3:00?

tomer is far greater than with a former customer or with a cold call.

Endorsements from outside of the organization of your prospect can also be valuable sales tools. Suppose, for example, that you worked with a large brokerage firm and recently completed a successful project. You can now use this experience to open the door at other brokerage firms. A potential script is presented in Figure 12-2. Once again, use the basic script with one minor modification. Use your past success to help you get the appointment. If you think about it, as long as you have completed one successful program at any company, you could try the third-party endorsement approach with other prospects. You will find that it will work quite well for you.

The final type of endorsement is the general third-party endorsement. I first discovered this tool when I was working in the mammoth corporate parks of New Jersey. Since New Jersey is quite spread out, it is not uncommon to visit four accounts in a day and put 200–300 miles on your car. Any salesperson in this territory must learn to make the best of his time. What I would find is that when I went to visit an account, there were often other large organizations either in the same corporate park or in the same general vicinity. Most salespeople would have a tape recorder in their car and would record the location of the account for later follow-up. I developed a more efficient approach, using third-party endorsements.

Walk into the offices of the other accounts unannounced

Figure 12-2. Second sample script for a "third party endorsement."

Mr. Davids please. Hello Mr. Davids. This is Teresa Smith of Exel Brokerage Services. How are you today? Great! The reason I'm calling is that we just completed a very successful project for Merrill Lynch. In fact, we provide brokerage services to many large organizations like yours. How do you handle your needs for those types of services at your company? Great! I'm going to be in your area on June 2 and would like to stop by and introduce myself. Are you available at 3:00?

---

and go up to the receptionist. Your discussion might proceed as outlined in Figure 12-3. This approach is similar to using a list without names and has just about as much success. It is a very effective method for learning the name of the definitive decision maker. You can follow up several days later for an appointment. A similar approach can be used at smaller branch offices of larger organizations, or even smaller companies, as long as they are in your target market. Here, the conversation would go exactly as the preceding one did except that you may ask the receptionist to distribute your product literature to everyone in the office. This would be particularly important if everyone in the office could use your product or service, or if you were trying to develop an overall awareness for your product or service. Try this latter approach if the office houses fifty employees or less. Receptionists in small offices tend to be very helpful. Be certain to note the receptionist's name because this, hopefully, will be

Figure 12-3. Face to face "third party endorsement" script.

Me:	Hello. My name is Paul Goldner of The Sales and Performance Group. I was wondering if you could help me.
Receptionist:	Sure.
Me:	Our company provides sales training to large companies like yours. In fact, we provide sales training to many of the major companies in the area. I was driving by and just happened to notice your company. I was wondering if you could tell me who would be responsible for purchasing sales training in your organization.
Receptionist:	Sure. That would be Mr. Travers.
Me:	Thank you. You have been most helpful. As long as I am here, I was wondering if you could do one other small favor for me.
Receptionist:	Sure. What can I do to help?
Me:	I was wondering if you could deliver this package to Mr. Travers.
Receptionist:	Why not.
Me:	I'm sorry, but I didn't ask your name.
Receptionist:	Sally Smith.
Me:	Sally, you've been most helpful. Thank you.

the beginning of a long relationship with her. Go back periodi-
cally to distribute product literature. Until you can develop a
firm relationship with a true decision maker, this individual will
be your internal champion, to represent your cause when you
are not there.

Third-party endorsements represent an excellent opportunity to leverage your success at a particular account and to leverage your success as a salesperson. At this point, we have
outlined an in-depth strategy for prospecting, cold calling, and
business development. The final step in the process is to learn
how to effectively track our progress, the subject of the next
chapter.

13

Tracking
Your Progress

The final element in your sales success formula is tracking your progress. Tracking your progress is important to your overall success, because if you track your progress, you can fine-tune your plans along the way. Sales reporting will allow you to understand your respective strengths and weaknesses. However, sales reporting has both pros and cons.

Arguments Against Sales Reporting

I will concede that sales reporting is time consuming. The classic argument against sales reporting is that it takes away valuable selling time. Although this may be true, sales reporting can also be a valuable coaching tool and a tool used for strategic planning. I prefer to view sales reporting as an investment in my own success. Sales reporting ensures that you are working smart. Sales reporting also requires attention to detail, a skill that is not a staple characteristic of most salespeople. On the other hand, without this attention to detail, you may overlook many items that are vital to your success. For example, assume that you continue to make call after call and never reach the decision maker you are targeting. A well-defined sales reporting form will identify this trend and tell you that you may want to consider changing your source of leads. Sales reporting can also be complicated. This is typically a function of the form. If the sales reporting system is complicated, make it simpler.

Arguments Supporting Sales Reporting

Now that we have reviewed, and hopefully overcome, some of the negative elements of sales reporting, let's take a look at some of the benefits, including sales forecasting and identifying areas for improvement. The pros far outweigh the cons, making sales reporting a skill worth learning to do well. Perhaps the most pervasive benefit of sales reporting is that it predicts future demand for your product or service. It is no secret that salespeople are not fond of preparing sales forecasts. Since reports create accountability, the salesperson may be required to live up to his projections. If salespeople are required to live up to their projections, there may be a tendency to underestimate their capabilities. This way they are sure to meet their plan. On the other hand, consistently underestimating demand will not provide management with the necessary information to allocate resources and make capital expenditures. In other words, it is in your best interest to accurately estimate demand, so you receive enough resources to meet the demands of your accounts. There is nothing as frustrating to a salesperson as selling an order and not having the product in place to meet customer demand. Accurate sales forecasts will help management to project demand for your product or service and have sufficient inventory or resources in place to meet the needs of your customers. Of course, you don't want to be overly optimistic in your projections either. Here, management will overallocate resources and the company will wind up making bad investment decisions. Nobody wins when the company makes bad investment decisions.

Sales reporting can also quantify the relationships among dials, completed calls, appointments, proposals, and ultimately sales. These performance trackers in turn indicate, for both management and yourself, opportunities for improvement. Chapter 2 established the very valuable relationship between dials of the telephone and income. Figure 13-1, again, outlines these relationships. Please note that the relationships implied in Figure 13-1 are for illustration purposes only. Your exact relationships depend on your industry, the list you are using for your cold

Figure 13-1. Information from a weekly sales report, reprise.

Dials	Completed Calls	Appointments	Proposals	Sales	Sales $
100	50	13	13	5	$20,000

calls, and your cold calling prowess. The only way you can determine your exact relationships is by keeping track of your cold calling activities over a long period of time. However, for illustration purposes, suppose that 50 percent of dials should lead to completed calls, but your ratio is only 25 percent. What does this mean? It could mean that you are not using a good or current list in your cold calling efforts. It could also mean that you are not calling at a good time and you may want to consider another time or varying your call times. The crucial point is that sales reporting can be a valuable feedback mechanism that will help you operate a peak performance.

Sales reporting also monitors goal attainment. As I mentioned earlier in this book, I am an avid Weight Watcher. I lost a lot of weight on the program, and over the years, I noticed one very interesting phenomenon. When I knew I would be going to Weight Watchers on Sunday morning in order to get weighed, I was religious about the program during the week. Consequently, I lost weight. On weeks when I knew that I would be out of town and would miss the dreaded Sunday morning weigh-in, I deviated from the program and usually gained weight. The point is, what gets measured, gets done. What doesn't, gets forgotten. When things are going well, one always has the tendency to pull back and smell the roses. The problem is that when you are smelling roses, someone else is working with your accounts and prospects. Weekly record keeping will keep your challenges alive, because each week you start with a clean slate. The likelihood of slacking off will be greatly diminished. An added benefit of measuring your results is that it will help build your cold calling confidence by proving that you make money each and every time you dial the telephone and that you have the ability to set your own level of income.

Your Sales Tracking Form

To record your sales prospecting activities, use a weekly sales tracking form such as the one presented in Figure 13-2. The form has five key segments: prospecting activity, meeting activity, pipeline activity, sales activity, and other pertinent information. The key elements of this form are explained below:

Dials: Record how many times you dial the phone in order to reach a decision maker for your product or service.

Figure 13-2. Sample weekly sales tracking form.

XYZ Company
Weekly Sales Report

Prepared by: _____   **Date:** _____

Prospecting Activity:

Day	Dials	Completed Calls	Appoint-ments	Recommen-dations	Sales	Sales Dollars
Monday						
Tuesday						
Wednesday						
Thursday						
Friday						
Total						
Percent*						

*Calculated as percent of previous column.

Meeting Activity:

Client	DDM	Date	Objective	Achievement	Stage of SC

DDM = Definitive Decision Maker. SC = Sales Cycle.

Pipeline Activity:

Client	Magnitude of Opportunity	Expected Close Date

(continues)

Figure 13-2. (*continued*)

Sales Activity:

Week	Weekly Sales	MTD Sales	Monthly Goal	% of Goal
One				
Two				
Three				
Four				

MTD = Month to Date

Other Pertinent Information:

_____

_____

_____

_____

_____

_____

_____

_____

_____

_____

_____

_____

Completed Calls:	Record the number of times that you reach the person you are dialing.
Appointments:	Record the number of appointments you receive from your completed calls.
Recommendations:	Record the number of proposals you issue as a result of your appointments or meetings.
Sales:	Record the number of winning proposals you issue.
Sales Dollars:	Record the dollar value of the sales from the previous column.
Total:	Record the sum of all the activity in each column for the week.
Percent:	Use this row to establish the weekly relationship between your various sales activities. In the Dials column record the percentage of dials that were completed calls. In the Completed Calls column record appointments as a percent of completed calls. In the Appointments column show proposals as a percent of appointments. Finally, include the percent of proposals that resulted in sales in the Recommendations column. Over time these ratios will normalize and you will have a very reliable predictor of your sales activities.

By way of example, the ratios for Sara Jones might appear as presented in Figure 13-3. Consider using these results as target ratios for your cold calling activities. If you are not able to achieve the same results as Sara's, you may need to make some changes in your strategy. For example, every two times Sara dials the phone, she completes one call (50 percent). If your rate is lower, consider changing your list or the times at which you make your calls. To improve your appointment ratio you need to work on your telephone skills. Review the Ten Command-

Figure 13-3. Sample business development benchmarks.

Dials	Completed Calls	Appointments	Proposals	Sales
2	1			
	4	1		
		1	1	
			2–3	1

ments of Prospecting and your cold calling scripts. You should always strive to issue a proposal or set of recommendations after every meeting. A prospect is meeting with you because she has a need. Your job is to uncover the need and develop a solution. Therefore, your ratio of meetings to proposals should be close to one-to-one. The proposal need not be a long and detailed document. A one-page letter might be sufficient. However, make certain you offer the prospect something she can purchase.

In our example, Sara makes one sale for every three proposals she develops. Although this result may be different than what you can expect in your industry, to improve your results consider seminars in consultative selling and/or proposal writing. You need to increase your understanding of the customer's needs and more effectively present your recommendations.

Finally, consider how these overall numbers can help you plan your cold calling strategies. Based on our example, consider that it should take twenty dials of the phone to make one sale. Further, you should be able to make these twenty calls in one hour. Therefore, if you want to make one sale per day, you need to prospect one hour per day. To increase sales production, you must increase your prospecting production. The relationship is that simple.

Over time, you will develop a feel for your sales ratios. You can also learn about your sales skills relative to those of your co-workers by comparing your ratios to theirs. I am not sure if sharing sales ratios will be common practice in your office; however, it would be quite beneficial to all who participate. In this manner, you could develop company and industry norms and have all members on the sales team strive to equal and exceed those norms.

The second and third components of your sales tracking form are used to track Meeting Activity and Pipeline Activity (see Figure 13-2). Your planned meeting activity results in your future sales or future income. If your inventory of appointments or opportunity runs too low, you can surely expect to have an income drought sometime thereafter. Pipeline activity is designed to measure your imminent sales. These are significant sales that you should expect to close in the near future. The next segment, Sales Activity, measures your sales production on both a weekly and monthly basis. The final portion of the form, Other Pertinent Information, is designed to reflect additional information that you believe is important to management or yourself and is not captured in other areas of the report.

Save your weekly tracking reports. When you are going through a strong period of high sales, look back and review your prior prospecting activity. Likewise, if you are going through a period of slower sales, look back and see why. In both cases, reflect on the Law of Sowing and Reaping.

Our prospecting success formula started with overcoming the fear of rejection, continued by developing a number of strategies to enhance your probability of success in the sales cycle, and ended with tracking your progress. The only question that remains is, Will this formula work specifically for you?—and that is the subject of our Conclusion.

Conclusion

Final Thoughts: The Four Steps to Success

The Four Steps to Success are a simple goal attainment formula: Set goals. Have confidence. Be persistent. Have fun! This system will ensure that the recommendations set forth in this book work for you.

Step 1: Set Goals

In very simple terms, the need for goal setting can be summarized in one short sentence: If you don't know what you are shooting for, how are you going to hit your target? When you are setting your goals, set your sights high—extremely high. Don't worry about hitting your goals. If you don't reach them today, you'll come back tomorrow and try again. Never give up. Further, as you try harder and harder to move outside of your comfort zone, even your failures (that is, not reaching your goals) will exceed the successes of most others. As goal setting relates to prospecting and business development, strive to be the very best you can—the best in your industry. As you set your goals, reflect on Chapters 4 and 5.

Step 2: Have Confidence

When I teach my Four Steps to Success seminar to inner-city high school kids I always start the session with one question: Who wants to be a success? The answer is always the same. A 100 percent positive response. Everyone wants to be a success. I go around the room and find that some of the kids want to be

Michael Jordan, others Oprah Winfrey, others Bill Clinton, and still others want to be doctors and lawyers—all very admirable goals, indeed.

However, when I ask how many think they can achieve their life's ambition, I always get a disappointing 10–20 percent positive response. I then tell a story of an experience that I had thirty years ago, when teaching this very same seminar in Little Rock, Arkansas.

The session in Little Rock started just the same as every other seminar, by asking the kids, "Who wants to be a success?" Just as I find today, I received a 100 percent response. As I went around the room and asked the kids what they wanted to be when they grew up, the answers were the same: doctors, lawyers, and stars of stage and screen, with one exception. There was a little kid in the class, Bill, who proudly declared that when he grew up, he wanted to be president of the United States. As expected, all of the kids laughed at Bill. However, when you think about it, his ambition to be president of the United States was not as farfetched as it might have seemed at the time. Each generation must produce its leaders. As long as someone has to do the job, why shouldn't it be you? Have the confidence to live your dreams. In developing your dreams, to be the best salesperson in your industry, reflect on Commandment 9.

Step 3: Be Persistent

It's very simple to look at a successful person and think how easy that person's success was achieved. However, most of us take the same road to success: hard work, many failures, and much persistence. Author Napoleon Hill said, "Within every failure is the seed of an equal or greater opportunity." Further, he noted that most great successes in life occur just after one's greatest defeat. Truer words have never been spoken.

Perhaps the greatest success story that I have ever read is the story of Victor Frankl, a prisoner in a Nazi death camp for many years. His book, *Man's Search for Meaning,* teaches the true meaning of persistence. Victor Frankl was able to endure the horrors of the Nazi death camps motivated by the dream of being reunited with his family at the end of the war. It's amazing what one man can endure, yet so many of us want to give up after far smaller defeats. As business developers, our greatest challenge is only to overcome telephone rejection. Persist—and remember Commandment 10.

Step 4: Have Fun

The great secret of prospecting is also the secret to life's success. **Have fun!** That's it. While most people dread prospecting, you shouldn't. Learn to love it. Prospecting is not work; it's play. You must enjoy doing something in order to do it well. How do you think Wayne Gretzky feels about playing hockey or Pete Sampras about playing tennis? I know neither of these individuals, but I bet I can guess the answer. Remember: Have fun.

Bibliography

Carnegie, Dale. *How to Win Friends and Influence People.* New York: Simon & Schuster, 1981.

Covey, Stephen R. *The Seven Habits of Highly Effective People: Restoring the Character Ethic.* New York: Fireside Books, 1989.

Frankl, Victor E. *Man's Search for Meaning: Revised and Updated.* New York: Washington Square Press, 1985.

Hill, Napoleon. *Think and Grow Rich.* New York: Fawcett Crest, 1960.

Karasik, Paul. *How to Make It Big in the Seminar Business.* New York: McGraw-Hill, Inc., 1992.

Mackay, Harvey. *Swim With the Sharks Without Being Eaten Alive: Outsell, Outmanage, Outmotivate, & Outnegotiate Your Competition.* New York: William Morrow & Co., 1988.

Index